Navigation for the Internet and other **Digital Media**
Studio **7.5**

Published by AVA Publishing SA
rue du Bugnon 7
CH-1299 Crans-près-Céligny
Switzerland
Tel: +41 786 005 109
Email: enquiries@avabooks.ch

Distruted by Thames and Hudson (ex-North America)
181a High Holborn
London WC1V 7QX
United Kingdom
Tel: +44 20 7845 5000
fax: +44 20 7845 5050
Email: sales@thameshudson.co.uk
www.thameshudson.com

Distributed by Sterling Publishing Co., Inc.
in USA
387 Park Avenue South
New York, NY 10016-8810
Tel: +1 212 532 7160
Fax: +1 212 213 2495
www.sterlingpub.com

in Canada
Sterling Publishing
c/o Canadian Manda Group
One Atlantic Avenue, Suite 105
Toronto, Ontario M6K 3E7

English Language Support Office
AVA Publishing (UK) Ltd.
Tel: +44 1903 204 455
Email: enquiries@avabooks.co.uk

Copyright © AVA Publishing SA 2002

ISBN 2-88479-011-X

10 9 8 7 6 5 4 3 2 1

Design by Studio **7.5**
Translation by Victor Dewsbery, Berlin

Production and separations by
AVA Book Production Pte. Ltd., Singapore
Tel: +65 6334 8173
Fax: +65 6334 0752
Email: production@avabooks.com.sg

AVA Publishing SA
Switzerland

Sterling Publishing Co., Inc.
New York

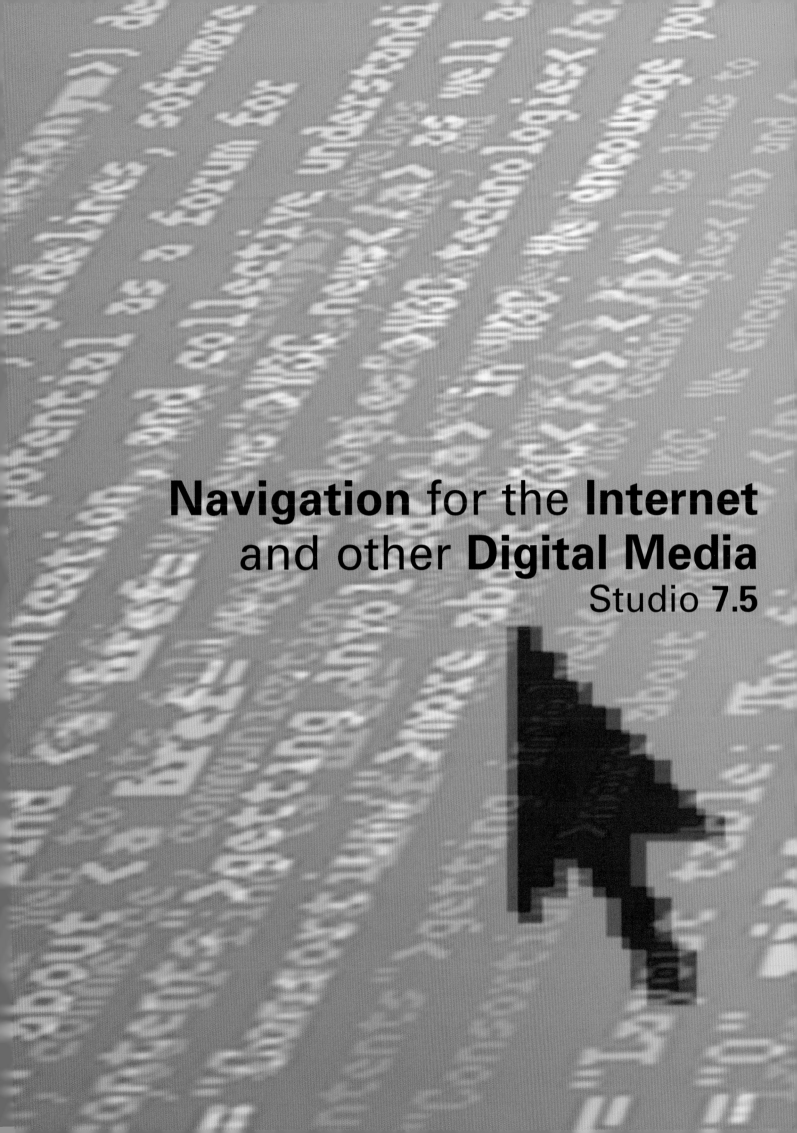

Content

: Introduction   8|9
: How to get the most out of this book   10|11

: Cognition and Recognition   60|75
Our senses can deal with many pieces of information at the same time. To enable us to grasp complex information quickly, visualisation is an important feature.
Visual, synchronous optical processing of data in real-time is the next challenge for the Internet. This chapter shows websites which already work on this principle.

: What is Navigation?   12|27
Strategies to discover and explore unknown territory.
This chapter shows the basic equipment that is needed to navigate the virtual world. Here you will find a compass, maps and other aids, like Ariadne's thread, to help you find your way on the Internet.

: Archetypes and Stereotypes   44|59
This is about the communication standards that have become established in the Internet. They are the rituals and design conventions in the World Wide Web. These conventions provide guidance, but sometimes these standards inhibit the forms of expression on the Internet.

: Navigation through Interaction   28|
An efficient system offers permanent feedback and thus preserves the context of the information. This gives the user the maximum freedom to make his own decisions. Highly developed applications can only be operated because they offer maximum feedback and thus enable the user to act quickly – and to correct any mistakes without delay. They show the direction in which the Internet will develop.

: New Frontiers 128|143

Here you will find examples of websites
which really use the potential of the Internet
as a medium and set new standards for
innovative interaction and navigation.

: Mental Models, Metaphors and Cyberworlds 108|127

Metaphors can help navigation. But not all the necessary
instructions for action can be deduced from them.
A logical navigation concept does not develop automatically.
Cyberworlds can be used as a bridge between the real
and the virtual world.

: Search Engines versus Serendipity 76|91

How do search engines search and what are their limits?
This chapter shows what can be found with the help of
a search engine and what can be stumbled upon
on the Internet without ever looking for it.
A day in the life of an Internet surfer.

1   2   3   4   5   6   7   8   9

: The Parallel Universe 92|107

The shop, the book, the daily newspaper,
the travel agent. There are specific navigation
techniques for different services on the
Internet. There are advantages for virtual
facilities, even if they sometimes merely
copy their real models.

: What´s Next? 144|153

On-line, everywhere and at all times.
How will the content and presentation of
the Internet change when the classical
screen is just one of many possible output
media, and when all electronic devices are
always on-line?

: Sources 154|155
: Acknowledgements 156|157
: Index 158|159

Introduction

What is "the Web"? What opportunities does it offer? What role will it play and how will it affect our way of life and our working habits? These are subjects of controversial discussion. In fact, the potential of the Internet is often overestimated or underestimated, and this is reflected in the extreme swing that is observed in the Nasdaq and other technology markets.

In the meantime, the medium of the Internet continues to develop dynamically and offers a flood of information and new services which are growing every day. The essence of a network is its decentralised, unco-ordinated organisation. This makes the Internet an exciting and extremely varied place. But it also means that the lack of a clear structure is immanent to the system. This makes it difficult for users to find their way.

| 1 | 2 | 3 | 4 | 5 | 6 | 7 | 8 | 9 |

This book illuminates the subject of navigation on the Internet in its many facets. This book is phenomenologically sub-divided into nine chapters and presents the various factors which make navigation on the Internet a pleasure or a chaotic rambling. What communication standards have already become established in the Internet which offer recognition and thus guidance?

What influence have transmission times and interactive elements on the ability to manoeuvre in the Internet? Can techniques such as metaphors and mental models offer a comprehensive navigation concept? How do different Internet services and applications, such as commerce, museums and daily newspapers, differ in their specific navigation techniques? How can search engines be used, and what are their limits?

Sites which are especially visionary in their navigation and provide an insight into the possible future of the Internet round off this general overview and make it a comprehensive collection for all involved in designing for the Internet.

How to get the most out of this book

Why a book? The subject of navigation on the Internet is a difficult one. First of all, it appears an anachronism to deal with this, of all subjects in the form of a book. A transient and fast-living medium which has at least four dimensions. How can it possibly be dealt with in a book?

On closer examination, however, some of these arguments actually work the other way. The transience of the medium means that valuable and interesting design ventures disappear more quickly than expected. What appears to be the obvious solution, creating a website with lists of links, will quickly be outdated.

But the really convincing argument for a book is different again: here it is possible to show many solutions alongside each other, i.e. in a **synchronous optical presentation**. It enables the user to see beyond the specific individual designs, to recognise the underlying patterns.

This is one of the reasons why collecting material is a typical habit of designers.

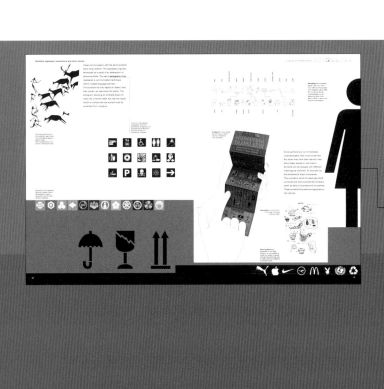

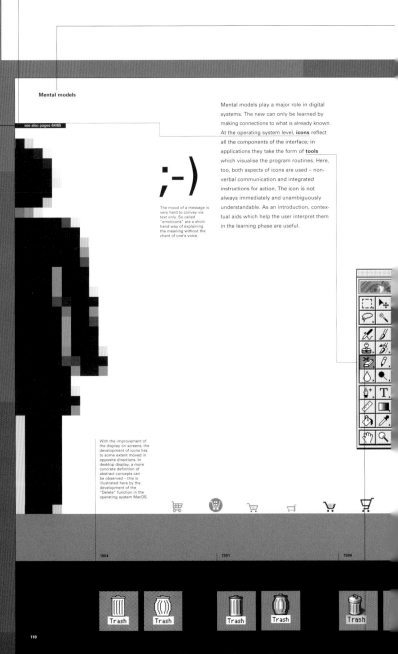

Mental models

see also pages 64/65

Mental models play a major role in digital systems. The new can only be learned by making connections to what is already known. At the operating system level, **icons** reflect all the components of the interface; in applications they take the form of **tools** which visualise the program routines. Here, too, both aspects of icons are used – nonverbal communication and integrated instructions for action. The icon is not always immediately and unambiguously understandable. As an introduction, contextual aids which help the user interpret them in the learning phase are useful.

The mood of a message is very hard to convey via text only. So called "emoticons" are a short-hand way of explaining the meaning without the chant of one's voice.

With the improvement of the display on screens, the development of icons has to some extent moved in opposite directions. In desktop display, a more concrete definition of abstract concepts can be observed – this is illustrated here by the development of the "Delete" function in the operating system MacOS.

How should the **nine chapters** be understood?
This is not a cookery book, nor a sequence
of lessons, nor can the chapters be separated
from each other. As with all complex subjects
in which we sense that everything is somehow
linked with everything else, the only solution
is to use various cross-sections to approach
the subject. It is only in this way that the
overlap that exists between areas of content
can heighten understanding rather than
create confusion.
The links between subjects are shown by
a **hyperlink system** on the pages, so it is
possible to follow a path that cuts across
the accustomed direction of reading.

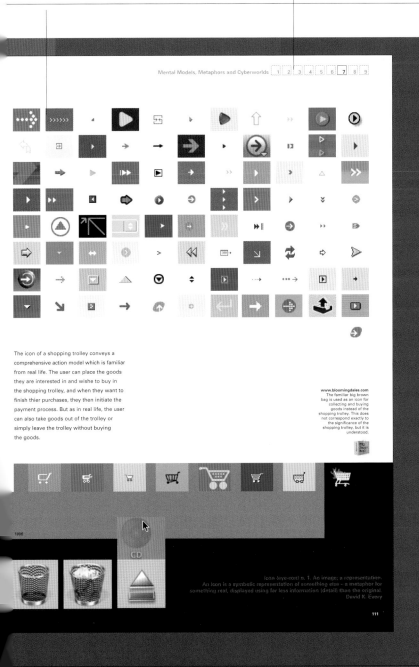

Mental Models, Metaphors and Cyberworlds 1 2 3 4 5 6 7 8 9

The icon of a shopping trolley conveys a
comprehensive action model which is familiar
from real life. The user can place the goods
they are interested in and wishe to buy in
the shopping trolley, and when they want to
finish thier purchases, they then initiate the
payment process. But as in real life, the user
can also take goods out of the trolley or
simply leave the trolley without buying
the goods.

www.bloomingdales.com
The familiar big brown
bag is used as an icon for
collecting and buying
goods instead of the
shopping trolley. This does
not correspond exactly to
the significance of the
shopping trolley, but it is
understood.

icon (eye-con) n. 1. An image; a representation.
An icon is a symbolic representation of something else – a metaphor for
something real, displayed using far less information (detail) than the original.
David K. Every

111

On the reading habits of designers:
This book uses hyperlinks to take into
account the changes in reading habits due
to the Internet. It also corresponds with the
perception of designers, which is mainly
dominated by the visual.

Text and pictures are shown as parallel
information paths; the content can also be
understood if the book is used as a picture
book only. This reading technique is supported
by the modular character of the content:
one double page, one thought. It is therefore
possible to start reading at any point and to
go on reading in any direction.

Even the fact that designers are impatient is
taken into account. Instead of a glossary in
the **appendix**, the concepts are explained
on the page by the addition of footnotes,
often visual.

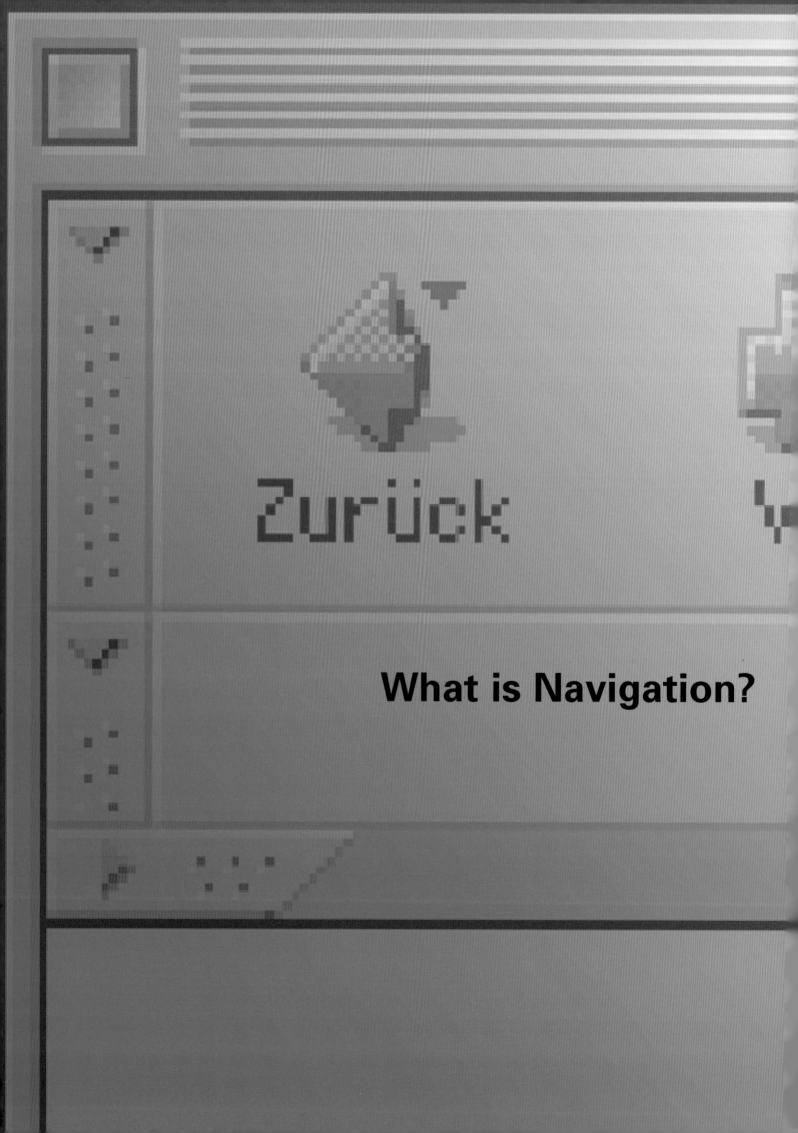

Zurück

What is Navigation?

Neu laden

An

1 2 3 4 5 6 7 8 9

How do we navigate in the real world? Can we draw any conclusions for navigation strategies in the virtual world? What starting points are there for the Internet? What can we learn from this to make sure that our site on the Internet is found?

Orientation in the real world

Orientation problems arise whenever our surroundings have very few features which can be used to get our bearings, for example on unknown terrain, in darkness, in the desert or at sea. A number of different navigation techniques have developed to enable us to find our way in spite of this. The word navigation is originally a seafaring term. Various tools are used for navigation. Maps are a miniature and abstract portrayal of reality. They help the user get his or her bearings. They show the world from a bird's-eye view.

There are a number of measuring instruments that we can use to determine our own position. In earlier times there were instruments such as sextants, and today there are satellite-guided GPS systems.

To make a return journey at any time and to find interesting items, we need some way to trace back the way we have come. **Marking** the way we have come and noting down interesting addresses is the most important navigation technique on the Internet. Links that we have already visited are marked in colour, and text is more or less "read into fragments".

Navigation instruments to determine where we are: sextant and GPS.

Plan of the "subway" in and around New York.

Go

Back	⌘[
Forward	⌘]
Home	⌘home

✓ Amazon.com: DVD / Genres / Kids & Family / Animati...
Amazon.com: buying info: Shrek
Amazon.com DVD
Amazon.com--Earth's Biggest Selection
http://www.lycos.com/
Video & DVD
Video & DVD
Barnes⊻&⊻Noble.com
Barnes⊻&⊻Noble.com College Textbooks Homepage
Wired Reprints
Wired Reprints: The Wired World Atlas
Wired Reprints
Wired Magazine Issue 10.01
Wired Magazine
Wired Magazine
Google-Suche: wired
Google

Borrowed from navigation techniques in the real world: the list of pages visited is a trail of digital "bread crumbs" which enables us to trace back the path we have trodden through the virtual world.

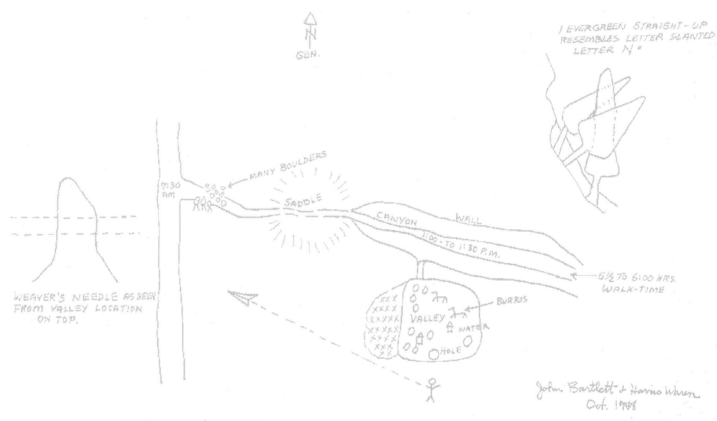

Gold prospector's sketched map dating from 1948.

In the fairy tale, "Hansel and Gretel" the children used the navigation principle of marking their own path with bread crumbs.

Ariadne's thread as a tool to find the way out of the Minotaur's labyrinth.

Orientation in information space: the book

The book as an information medium, with its physical dimension, conveys a considerable amount of context information which we do not have in the digital world. The thickness of the book, for example, shows how extensive the content is. We can clearly identify where the book begins and where it ends.

This follows the writer's suggestion for the order in which the information provided should best be read. We can see how far we have got through the book by looking at the two halves of the opened book.

The book as a communication medium has many centuries of tradition in which reading habits and design rules have developed. If we disregard the deviations which have arisen from different speech and writing cultures, the reader has a clear expectation for the navigation elements such as headings, **page numbers** and the table of contents.

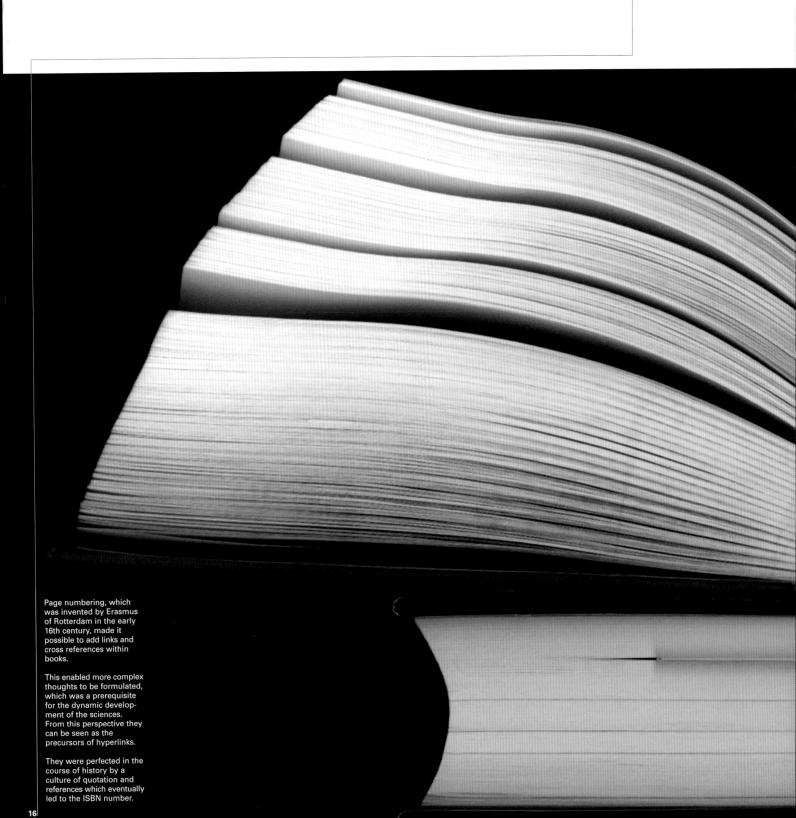

Page numbering, which was invented by Erasmus of Rotterdam in the early 16th century, made it possible to add links and cross references within books.

This enabled more complex thoughts to be formulated, which was a prerequisite for the dynamic development of the sciences. From this perspective they can be seen as the precursors of hyperlinks.

They were perfected in the course of history by a culture of quotation and references which eventually led to the ISBN number.

Bookmarks

Add Bookmark	⌘D
Edit Bookmarks	⌘B

Guide ▶

Personal Toolbar Folder
imke ▶
Persönliche Symbolleiste-Ordner
Live Home Page
Suchen
Macintosh Produktkatalog

Apple ▶
Unterstützung und Informationen ▶
Veröffentlichungen über Macintosh ▶
Hardware- und Software-Händler ▶
Software-Entwickler ▶
Hardware-Entwickler ▶
Multimedia ▶

Eigene Bookmarks
navibook ▶
index
Quark Incorporated
Quark: Download Results
Quark: Download Results
gravis.de – Coming home!
HotBot DE
Yahoo!
Sign in – Yahoo! Mail
lap6
Google
Dictionary Search Englisch-Deutsch
Langenscheidts Fremdwörterbuch online
Google
NewsMaps.com Shows Visual Landscapes of News
Free SpeedScript: the speedway to new DHTML and Ja...
Internet Einfuehrung
Google-Suche: webhistory
Google-Suche: webseiten wachstum
Suchmaschinen – Teoma
deutsche Suchmaschinen
Suchmaschinen Expertenportal wer-weiss-was, www.we...
Google-Suche: informationsflut
Kampf gegen die Informationsflut
menu.w3history.phtml
sources.de.phtml
Internet Domain Survey
Nua Internet Surveys : Graphs & Charts - 1998
Übersicht - Zahlen & Fakten
Internet Software Consortium - Number of Internet ...
~futurefarmers~
The Dell Store
▼

see also pages 90|91

Borrowed from the context
of books: the metaphor of
the bookmark, i.e. marking
interesting contents with
a bookmark or a dog-ear
to find it again more
easily later.

The IP (Internet Protocol) number, the actual address of the computer.

On the Internet we can travel with seven-league boots, and following a link can take us all around the world in five minutes. As there is no physical representation, we often do not know where we are at any given time, how much information we have already received and how much we may have missed. An analysis of the components of the URL we are visiting gives us at least some indication.

205.188.157.1

The HTTP (hypertext transfer protocol) enables browsers to display the pages that have been called up.

World Wide Web.

The domain name, in this case the Internet portal AOL.

The top level domain, in this case the domain .com, which stands for commercial content on the Web.

http://www.aol.com

This URL corresponds to the IP number shown above. So-called domain name servers provide the directories in which the IP numbers are linked with the corresponding names.

http://www.aol.com/cor

Sub-domains of the domain AOL.

http://my.screenname.a

There are no maps for the Internet which can provide direct assistance in navigation. There is cartographically processed information about the flow of traffic, the number of hosts and their worldwide distribution. There is no correlation to the respective content offered.

Visualisation of the data flow in May 1993 within the usenet.
E-net mapped by Brian Reid / DEC Western Research Labs.

Where there is a higher degree of networking, the information will take the same path less frequently and the neighbourhoods will be less relevant as a guideline for navigation. If we take into account the dynamic nature of the Internet, it is unlikely that the user will ever return to the same place a second time.

A sub-directory of the domain AOL, marked by a slash.
The meaningful name of the directory structures within a website makes self-explanatory URLs possible.

This is a file in HTML format in the directory **community** which can be interpreted by the browser.

unity/directory.html

Here, dynamic information is passed on together with the URL: Within the AOL portal the user can log in with a name and a password, and his or her specific settings are called up from the database with this dynamic URL.

om/_cqr/login/login.psp?e

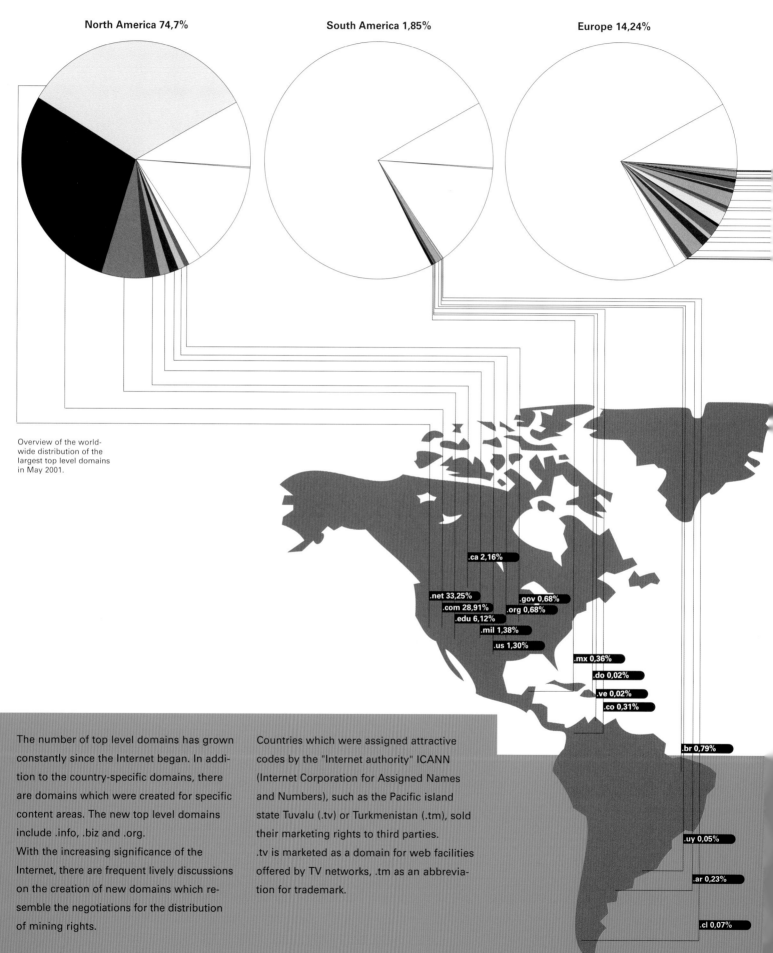

North America 74,7%

South America 1,85%

Europe 14,24%

Overview of the world-
wide distribution of the
largest top level domains
in May 2001.

.ca 2,16%

.net 33,25%
.com 28,91%
.edu 6,12%
.mil 1,38%
.us 1,30%

.gov 0,68%
.org 0,68%

.mx 0,36%

.do 0,02%

.ve 0,02%

.co 0,31%

.br 0,79%

.uy 0,05%

.ar 0,23%

.cl 0,07%

The number of top level domains has grown
constantly since the Internet began. In addition to the country-specific domains, there
are domains which were created for specific
content areas. The new top level domains
include .info, .biz and .org.
With the increasing significance of the
Internet, there are frequent lively discussions
on the creation of new domains which re-
semble the negotiations for the distribution
of mining rights.

Countries which were assigned attractive
codes by the "Internet authority" ICANN
(Internet Corporation for Assigned Names
and Numbers), such as the Pacific island
state Tuvalu (.tv) or Turkmenistan (.tm), sold
their marketing rights to third parties.
.tv is marketed as a domain for web facilities
offered by TV networks, .tm as an abbrevia-
tion for trademark.

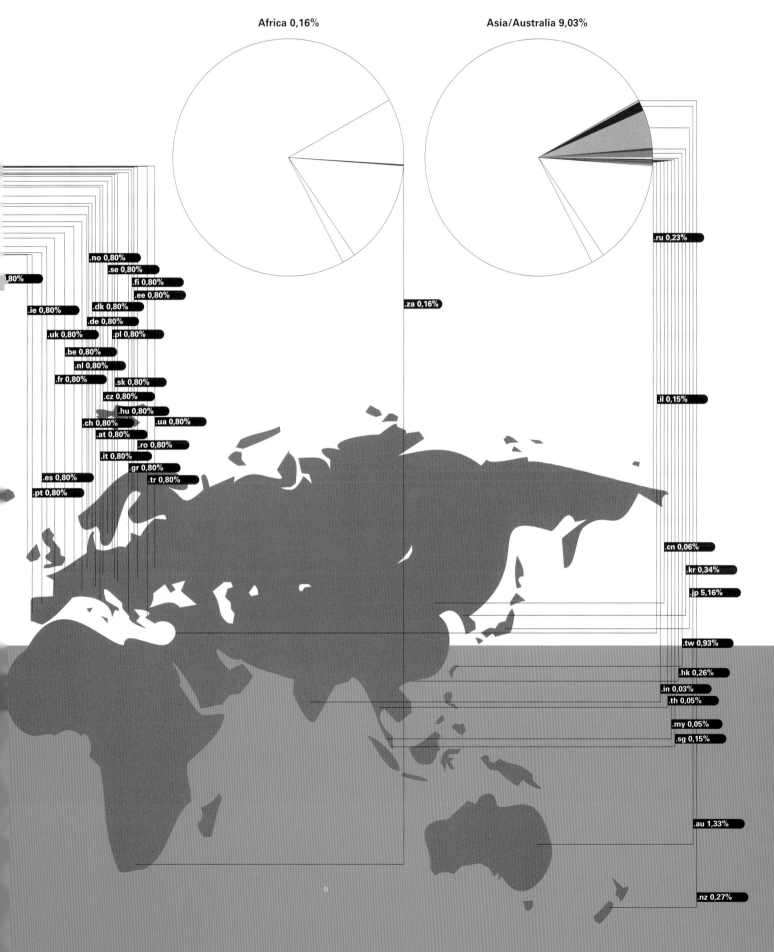

Africa 0,16%

Asia/Australia 9,03%

.no 0,80%
.se 0,80%
.fi 0,80%
.ee 0,80%
.80%
.ie 0,80%
.dk 0,80%
.de 0,80%
.uk 0,80%
.pl 0,80%
.be 0,80%
.nl 0,80%
.fr 0,80%
.sk 0,80%
.cz 0,80%
.hu 0,80%
.ch 0,80%
.ua 0,80%
.at 0,80%
.ro 0,80%
.it 0,80%
.gr 0,80%
.es 0,80%
.tr 0,80%
.pt 0,80%

.za 0,16%

.ru 0,23%
.il 0,15%
.cn 0,06%
.kr 0,34%
.jp 5,16%
.tw 0,93%
.hk 0,26%
.in 0,03%
.th 0,05%
.my 0,05%
.sg 0,15%
.au 1,33%
.nz 0,27%

The browser

The browser is the tool which is used to navigate on the Internet. Mosaic and its successor Netscape Navigator invented and defined the category of the browser. The browser forms the framework within which the pages are called up and the content is displayed.
The names of the two best known browsers, "Navigator" and "Explorer", remind us of the discovery of far away, unfamiliar territory.

Field to enter the URL. A widespread navigation method is guessing the URL.
Registering all meaningful domain names is a useful method to ensure that websites are found.

Mosaic 3.0

Navigator 4.7

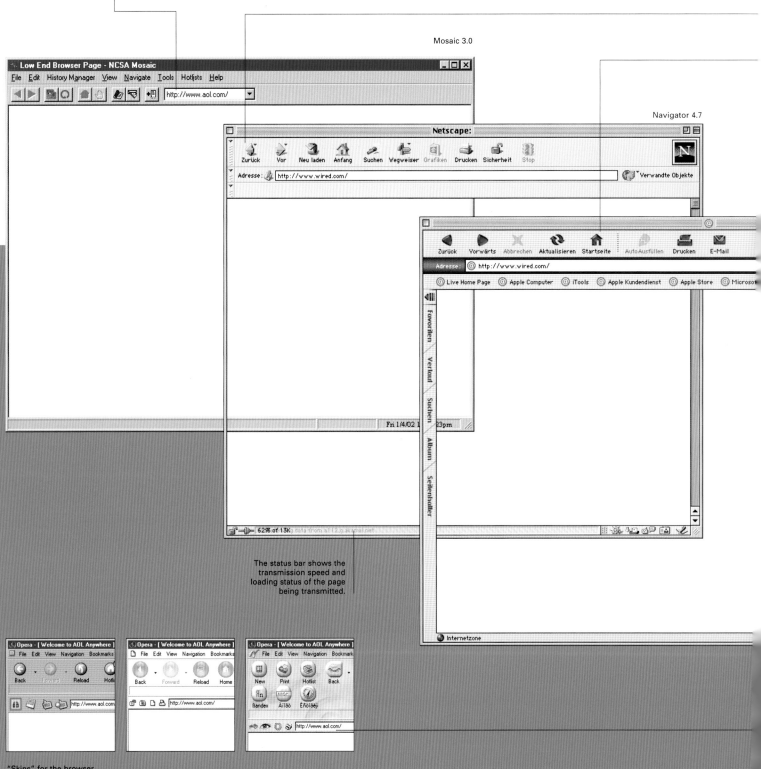

The status bar shows the transmission speed and loading status of the page being transmitted.

"Skins" for the browser **Opera 6.0**. The functions of the browser are standardised, the user can choose between various interfaces depending on his or her personal taste.

Little has changed in the basic functions since the development of the first visual browser "Mosaic". There is an entry field for the destination address and buttons that can be used to navigate **backwards** and forwards, and the button **"Home"** takes the user back to his chosen starting point at any time.

The stages of the journey can be retraced, and interesting addresses that the user has visited can be noted down as a bookmark. A status bar provides information about the loading speed. The **animated logo** visualises the Internet connection.

Explorer 5.0

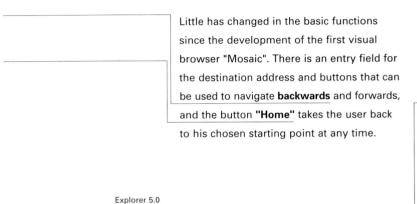

Opera Version 6.0

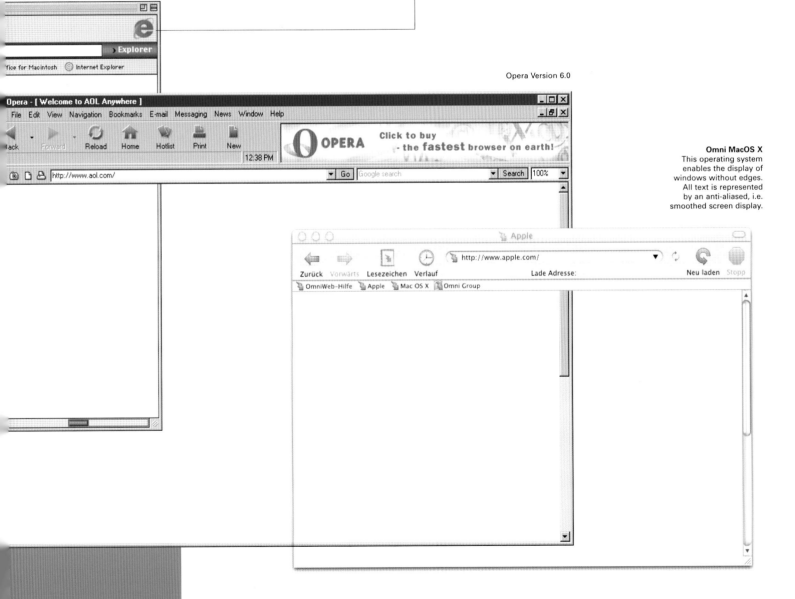

Omni MacOS X
This operating system enables the display of windows without edges. All text is represented by an anti-aliased, i.e. smoothed screen display.

Starting points on the Internet: the Internet portal

The size and variety of the Internet makes navigating to interesting targets difficult. Portals are a good starting point for a visit to the Internet. A portal offers a preselection of links and sites which make the choice easier for the user. In addition the user can configure the portal to cater for his or her own needs. For example, current weather reports corresponding to the user´s place of residence and other personal settings can be saved.

However, many portals suffer from the fact that they aim to serve as broad a target group as possible, which means that their services become arbitrary. No amount of adjustment to the configuration settings can significantly change this.
Portal concepts devoted to a specific target group are more suited to the medium.

www.military.com
Portal for military personnel

www.IgoUgo.com
Portal for globetrotters

www.AJkids.com
Portal for children

Another strategy to find interesting content is to use a "pilot" or guide. Complex sites offer their own pilot service to introduce users to their site; while Internet guides have also been developed which offer theme tours of the Internet.

www.datango.com
A service which offers navigation in the form of "guided tours" of websites.

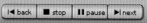

www.myNetscape.com
A configurable Internet portal offered by the Netscape company.
The user can select and arrange the information to suit his or her personal preferences.

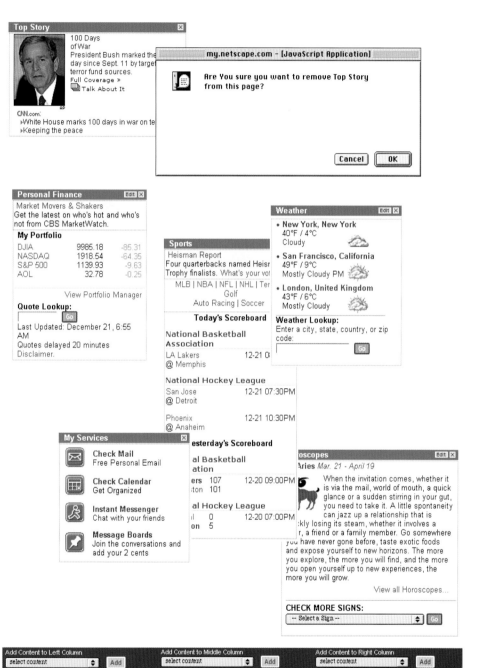

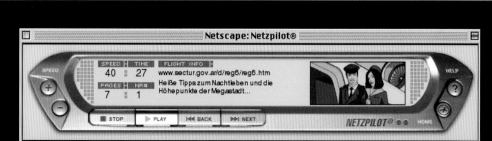

Cross-media references

The links between the real world and the virtual world are increasingly close. It is ever more common for extra information and service facilities to be offered when a www address is given. These addresses, which are found in all traditional media and increasingly also on products, are offered as systematic entrance points for the Internet.

www.dececco.it

www.bobmarley.com

www.ninewest.com

www.aveda.com

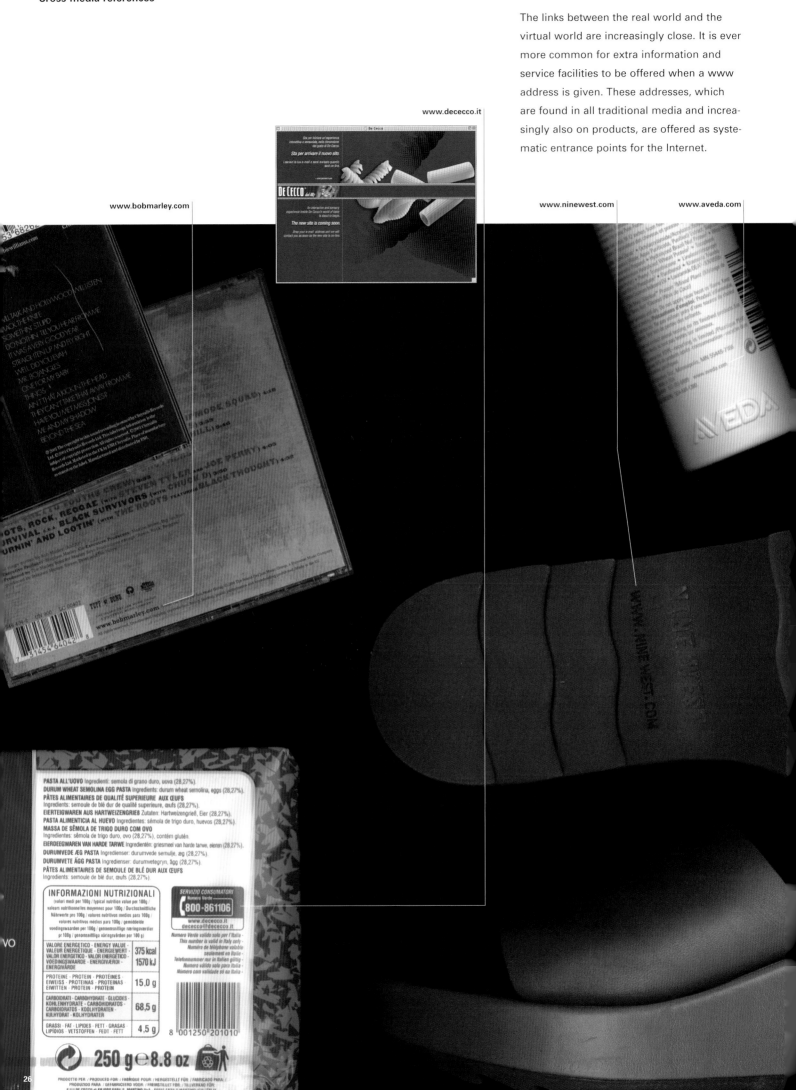

They form anchor points linking real objects
to dynamic digital information. These links
are possibly the precursors of bidirectional
networks and **networked products**.

see also pages 152|153

www.avabooks.co.uk | www.ft.com | www.ebrary.com

Navigation through Interaction

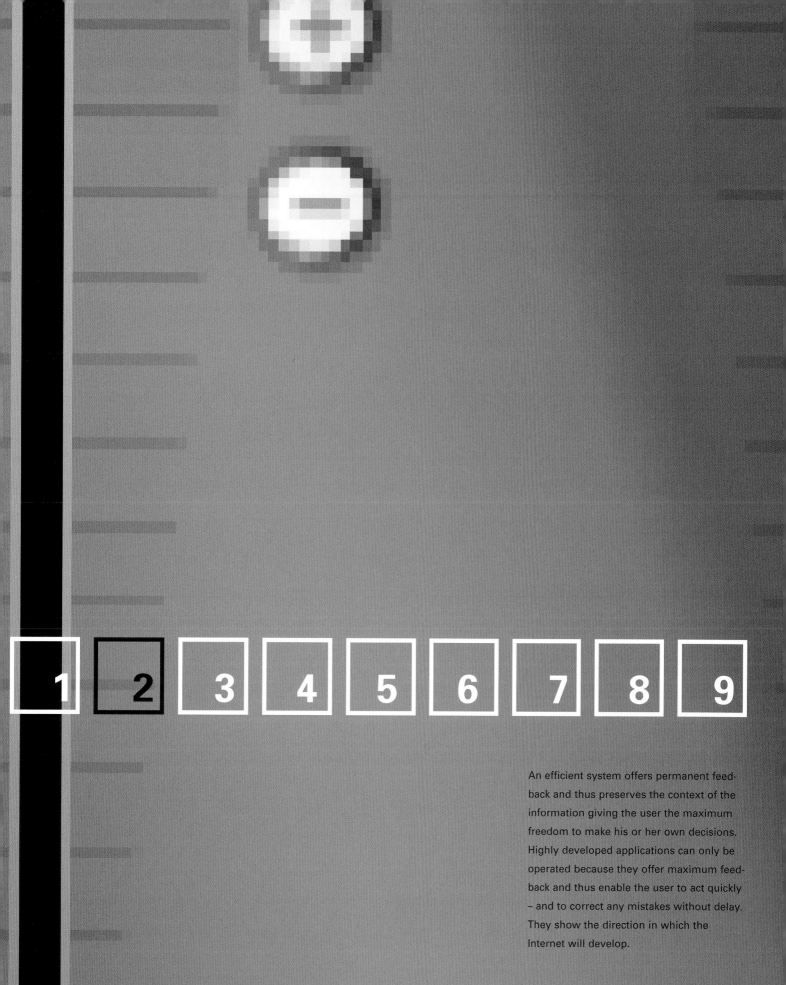

1 2 3 4 5 6 7 8 9

An efficient system offers permanent feedback and thus preserves the context of the
information giving the user the maximum
freedom to make his or her own decisions.
Highly developed applications can only be
operated because they offer maximum feedback and thus enable the user to act quickly
– and to correct any mistakes without delay.
They show the direction in which the
Internet will develop.

The interactive machine

The interface of modern computers with its graphic user interface, keyboard and mouse makes a variety of interactions possible between user and the computer. With the aid of the mouse the user can at least reach into the computer with one arm, point at elements and move them with his or her hand, represented by the cursor.

The computer registers and interprets all the movements of the user. Direct manipulation of the objects on the screen is the most intuitive form of interaction.

In addition, intuitive user surfaces stand out by the fact that they draw intelligent conclusions from the actions of the user. Users give simple instructions to the computer and trigger a chain of highly complex calculations, and the results are then represented visually and can be grasped intuitively by the user.

The "drafting assistant" in the CAD software Ashlar Vellum interprets the cursor movements and helps to find the points that are being looked for.

midpoint

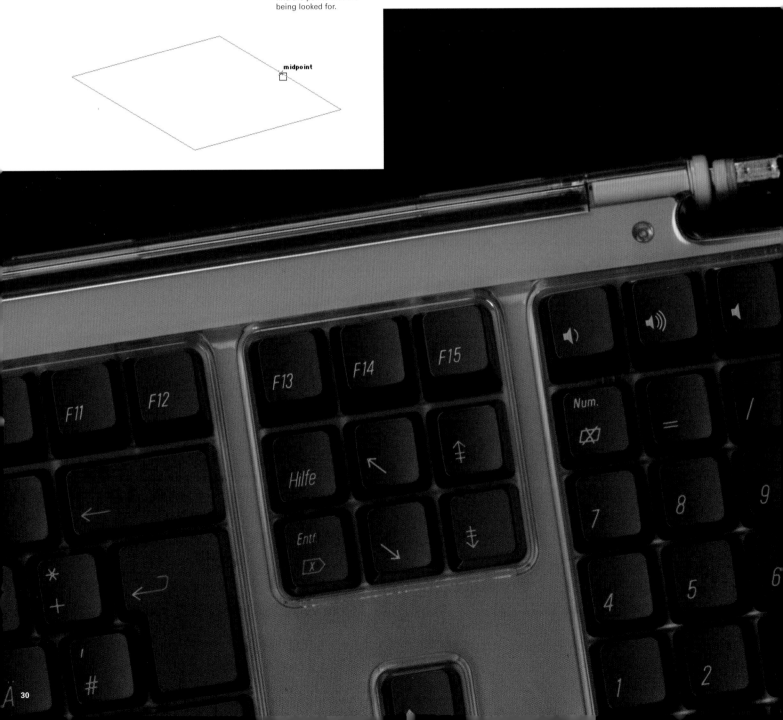

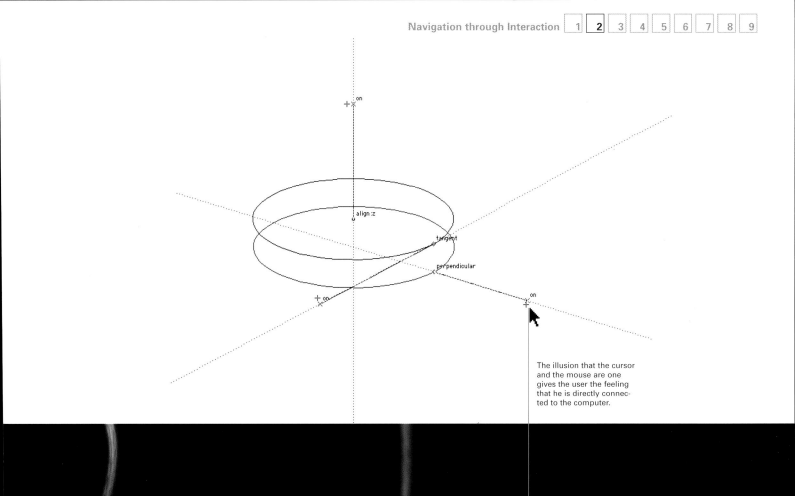

on

align :z

tangent

perpendicular

on

on

The illusion that the cursor
and the mouse are one
gives the user the feeling
that he is directly connected to the computer.

Feedback

Feedback from the computer is crucial for intuitive navigation. It could be described as the gravity of the virtual world.

The feedback between the action of the user and the reaction of the computer must be as direct as possible. This is necessary so that the user can evaluate and, if necessary, correct the effects of his own actions.

If there is a delay, the user loses touch with the computer. His actions overlap with the computer's reactions, but with a time lag. This leads to a misunderstanding between the user and the computer, and this can often cause the program to crash.

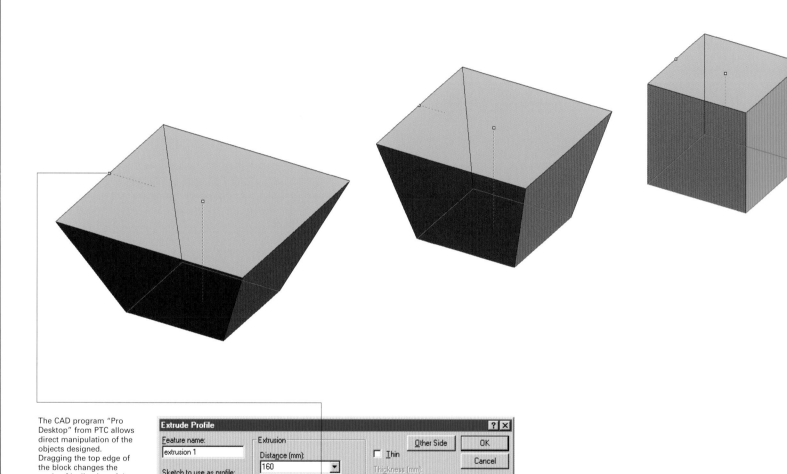

The CAD program "Pro Desktop" from PTC allows direct manipulation of the objects designed. Dragging the top edge of the block changes the angle of inclination of the side surfaces, and the exact value is constantly displayed in a control panel.

Extrude Profile

Feature name:
extrusion 1

Sketch to use as profile:
initial

- Add material
- Subtract material
- Intersect material

Extrusion

Distance (mm):
160

- Above workplane
- Below workplane
- Symmetric about workplane

Taper angle: -25

Thin
Thickness (mm):
0
Symmetric

Other Side
OK
Cancel
Preview
Calculator

56K analogue modem

ISDN
Integrated Services Digital Network

T-1 Line
Time-division multiplexing

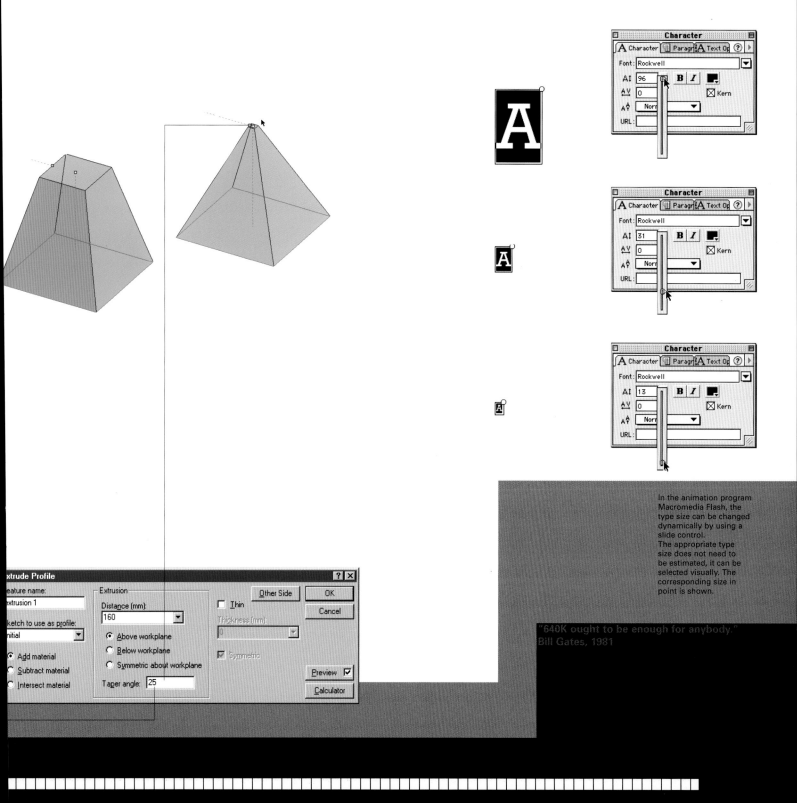

Extrude Profile

Feature name:
Extrusion 1

Sketch to use as profile:
Initial

○ Add material
○ Subtract material
○ Intersect material

Extrusion
Distance (mm):
160
☐ Thin
Thickness (mm):
0
● Above workplane
○ Below workplane
○ Symmetric about workplane
☑ Symmetric
Taper angle: 25

Other Side
OK
Cancel
Preview ☑
Calculator

In the animation program Macromedia Flash, the type size can be changed dynamically by using a slide control.
The appropriate type size does not need to be estimated, it can be selected visually. The corresponding size in point is shown.

"640K ought to be enough for anybody."
Bill Gates, 1981

Speed on the Internet depends on the parameter bandwidth, type of connection and traffic. This illustration shows the transfer time needed for one Megabyte of data using different types of connection.
(unit = one second)

The quality of the feedback is largely determined by the reaction speed of the system. This is not necessarily the same as the processor speed and transmission rate, but these two **parameters** certainly influence the agility of the system's reactions.

Hyperlinks and their pitfalls in navigation

Hyperlinks are associative leaps to related topics which are connected with the link. These leaps take the user out of the present context and transport him or her to a new position within the information. We could think of this as "riding the tube" within a website. The visitor always sees only a small extract and not the big picture. He or she has to remember the path taken and the things seen. The only help is the **colour coding** for the links already visited – as long as the Web designer has kept to this convention.

A decisive criterion for good orientation is the preservation of the context. Good navigation therefore means that the user must be able to make a **mental model** of the whole content. This is the user´s personal site plan which enables him or her to map what he or she has seen and find it again if necessary. Good websites offer such a model.

Homer and his world
Multimedia CD-ROM
Homer's life's work is presented here in zoomable form. The display does not jump when a link is clicked. Instead, there is a continuous movement to the next place in the text, so with this technique the user can always keep an eye on the path he or she has navigated.

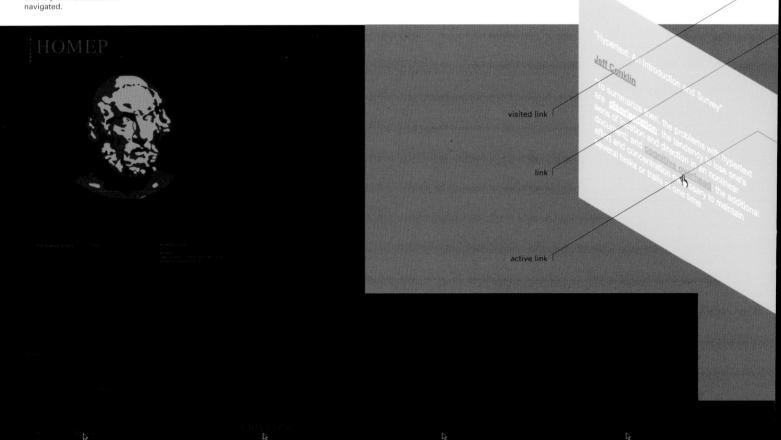

visited link

link

active link

"Hypertext: An Introduction and Survey"
Jeff Conklin

To summarize then: the problems with hypertext are disorientation: the tendency to lose one's sens of location and direction in an nonlinear document, and cognitive overhead: the additional effort and concentration necessary to maintain several tasks or trails at one time.

HOMEP

zwei eier sind eine einladung zu rührei

Der denkende Entwerfer und entwerfende Denker Otl Aicher

Invitation to scrambled eggs Multimedia CD-ROM The life and work of the designer Otl Aicher in a hypertext structure. The main text is always visible, and extra background information can be displayed as desired.

Projekt   Danke   Hallo

Otl Aicher gehörte zu den Gründern der Hochschule für Gestaltung (HfG) Ulm. Er prägte den Begriff „Erscheinungsbild", gestaltete die Olympischen Spiele 1972 und wurde damit weltweit bekannt.

Er zog in sein „autonomes rotis", arbeitete dort für Lufthansa, ERCO, FSB, Braun und das ZDF. Er entwarf auch eine Schriftfamilie: Die „Rotis". Außerdem schrieb er zahlreiche Bücher, die Einblick in sein Denken geben.

see also pages 110|111

see also pages 46|47

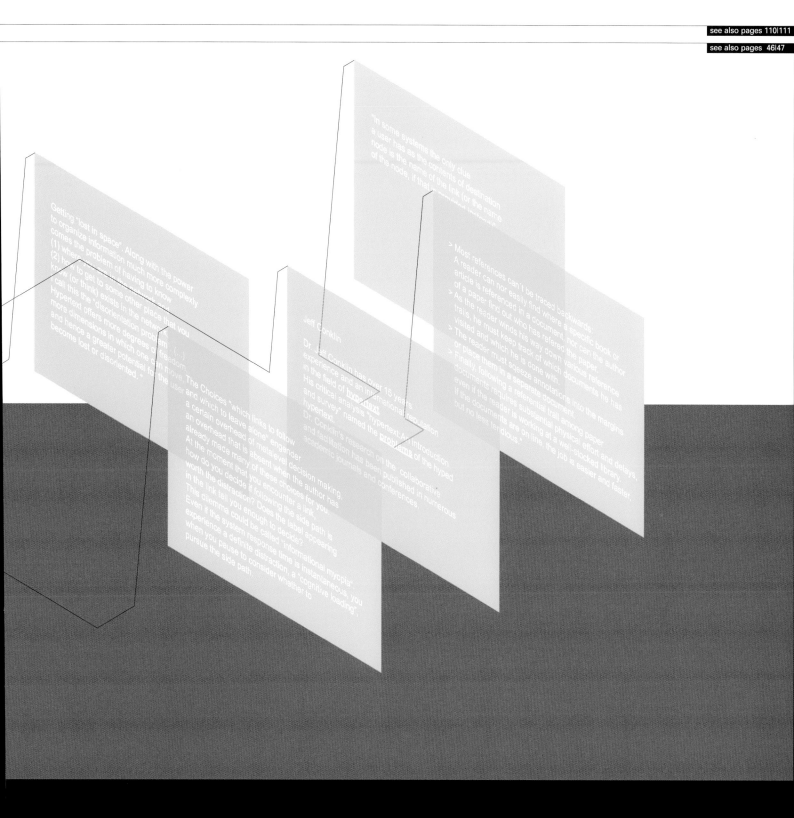

Otl Aicher gehörte zu den Gründern der Hochschule für Gestaltung (HfG) Ulm. Er prägte den Begriff "Erscheinungsbild", gestaltete die Olympischen Spiele 1972 und wurde damit weltweit bekannt.

Er zog in sein "autonomes Leben", arbeitete dort für Lufthansa, ERCO, FSB, Braun und das ZDF. Er entwarf auch eine Schriftfamilie: Die "Rotis". Außerdem schrieb er zahlreiche Bücher, die Einblick in sein Denken geben.

Otl Aicher, eigentlich Otto Aicher, wurde am 13. Mai 1922 in Ulm an der als Sohn eines Handwerkers geboren. Er war künstlerisch hochbegabt, philosophisch und literarisch interessiert. Das Erleben der Naziherrschaft prägte ihn. Von 1946 an studierte er zwei Jahre Bildhauerei an der Akademie der bildenden Künste in München. Schon 1948 gründete er sein eigenes graphisches Studio in Ulm.
Er lernte seine spätere Frau Inge Scholl kennen und heiratete sie 1952.
Neben seiner lebenslangen Beschäftigung mit Grafik und Design, wanderte Aicher leidenschaftlich in der Wüste.

Otl Aicher gehörte zu den Gründern der Hochschule für Gestaltung (HfG) Ulm. Er prägte den Begriff "Erscheinungsbild", gestaltete die Olympischen Spiele 1972 und wurde damit weltweit bekannt.

Er zog in sein "autonomes rotis", arbeitete dort für Lufthansa, ERCO, FSB, Braun und das ZDF. Er entwarf auch eine Schriftfamilie: Die "Rotis". Außerdem schrieb er zahlreiche Bücher, die Einblick in sein Denken geben.

Otl Aicher, eigentlich Otto Aicher, wurde am 13. Mai 1922 in Ulm an der als Sohn eines Handwerkers geboren. Er war künstlerisch hochbegabt, philosophisch und literarisch interessiert. Das Erleben der Naziherrschaft prägte ihn. Von 1946 an studierte er zwei Jahre Bildhauerei an der Akademie der bildenden Künste in München. Schon 1948 gründete er sein eigenes graphisches Studio in Ulm.
Er lernte seine spätere Frau Inge Scholl kennen und heiratete sie 1952.
Neben seiner lebenslangen Beschäftigung mit Grafik und Design, wanderte Aicher leidenschaftlich in der Wüste.

Otl Aicher gehörte zu den Gründern der Hochschule für Gestaltung (HfG) Ulm. Er prägte den Begriff "Erscheinungsbild", gestaltete die Olympischen Spiele 1972 und wurde damit weltweit bekannt.

Er zog in sein "autonomes rotis", arbeitete dort für Lufthansa, ERCO, FSB, Braun und das ZDF. Er entwarf auch eine Schriftfamilie: Die "Rotis". Außerdem schrieb er zahlreiche Bücher, die Einblick in sein Denken geben.

Inge Aicher-Scholl wurde am 11. August 1917 in Ingersheim geboren und machte eine Ausbildung als Prüfungsassistentin. Sie ist die älteste Schwester von Hans und Sophie Scholl, die im aktiven Widerstand gegen das NS-Regime als Mitglieder der Gruppe "Die Weiße Rose" umgebracht wurden.
Inge Aicher-Scholl gründete nach dem Krieg die Ulmer Volkshochschule und leitete sie zwischen 1946 und 1974. Sie gehört zu den Gründern der Ulmer Hochschule für Gestaltung; Die von ihr initiierte "Geschwister-Scholl-Stiftung" war Trägerin der HfG Ulm. Seit 1972 beschäftigt sie sich mit dem Archiv über ihre Geschwister und deren Widerstandsaktionen.

Spatial memory

Order in the real world means that you can find certain things again because you remember where you have put them.

Storing information on a surface or in a spatial environment is a reliable memory technique. You can find the information again by remembering where it is.

The representation of the complete content in the form of a general overview map which puts the content into a spatial context is a helpful navigation structure. To enable the user to keep his or her bearings, every movement must flow and the navigation must be continuous. This applies particularly to three-dimensional models.

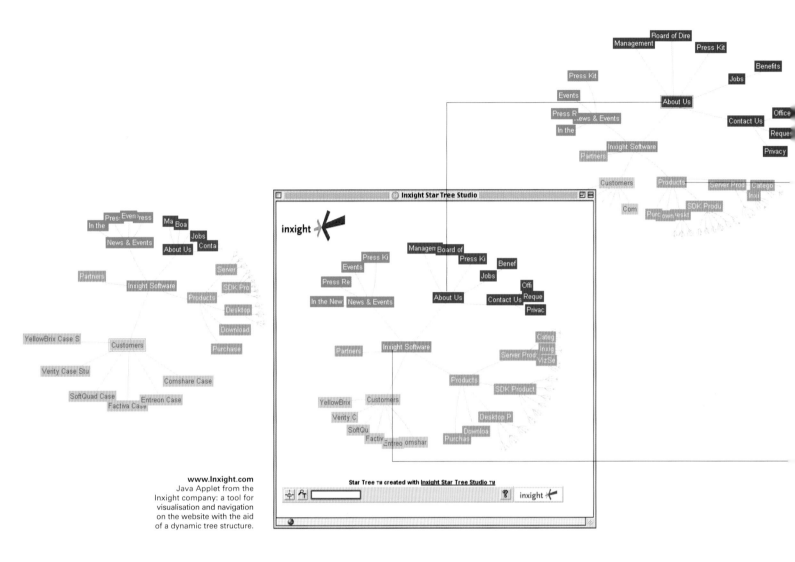

www.Inxight.com
Java Applet from the Inxight company: a tool for visualisation and navigation on the website with the aid of a dynamic tree structure.

Macromedia Freehand
The pages created are displayed in a navigator in their position on the desktop.

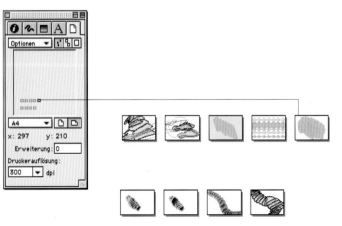

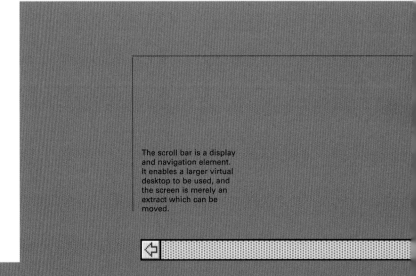

The scroll bar is a display and navigation element. It enables a larger virtual desktop to be used, and the screen is merely an extract which can be moved.

The writer Simonides of Keos (approx. 556–468 B.C.) is regarded as the "inventor" of memory techniques because he is mentioned in Roman rhetorics manuals.

At a banquet at which the festival hall suddenly collapsed and Simonides survived by some happy chance, he was the one who could identify the bodies because he had memorised the seating order of the guests. This experience convinced him that spatially arranged mental pictures are the best aid to memory.

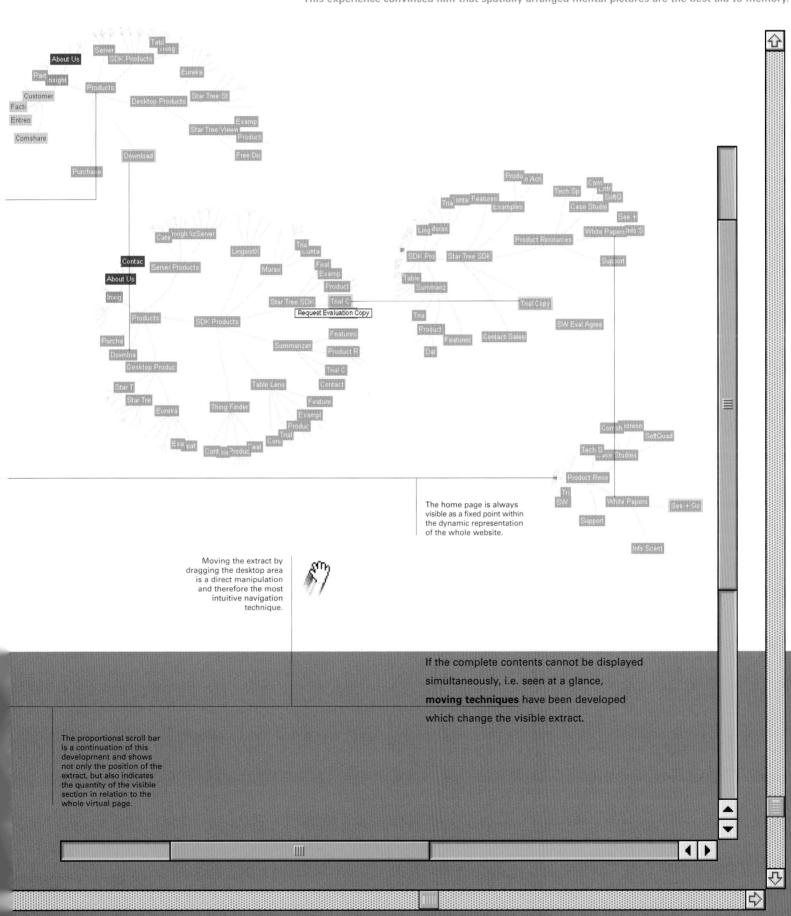

The home page is always visible as a fixed point within the dynamic representation of the whole website.

Moving the extract by dragging the desktop area is a direct manipulation and therefore the most intuitive navigation technique.

If the complete contents cannot be displayed simultaneously, i.e. seen at a glance, **moving techniques** have been developed which change the visible extract.

The proportional scroll bar is a continuation of this development and shows not only the position of the extract, but also indicates the quantity of the visible section in relation to the whole virtual page.

The time axis as a narrative framework

The arrangement of information based on its chronological order is a very robust navigation concept. In conjunction with the horizontal reading direction from left to right, it forms a mental model which can readily be understood.

The user must navigate to the left to reach the past, or to the right to reach the future.

A vertical orientation of a time bar is less common. Where it occurs, the present is the starting point, and the user can navigate down into the past or up into the future. Here, too, the fact that the limited size of the screen only allows the user to see an extract can be overcome by continuous navigation.

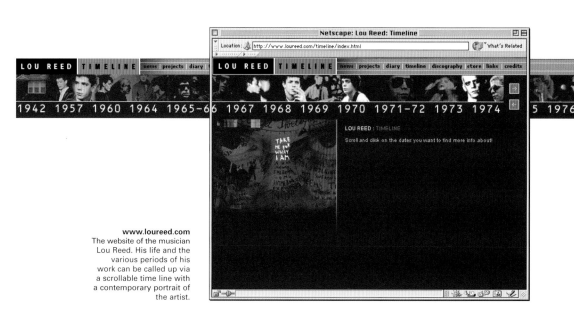

www.loureed.com
The website of the musician Lou Reed. His life and the various periods of his work can be called up via a scrollable time line with a contemporary portrait of the artist.

www.avantGo.com
The time line used as narrative framework for introducing a new software: A day in the life of a sales representative using this mobile office solution.

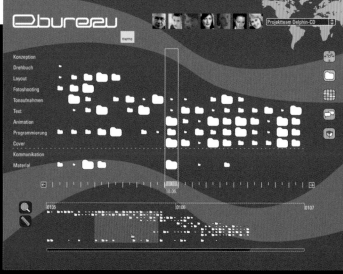

eBureau
Design concept for an Internet-based project work environment. The sequence of the project is documented with a time line and can be viewed at two different zoom settings.

1064

1087

The Bayeux Tapestry
One of the first synchronous optical representations of an event. The conquest of England by the Normans takes the form of a 70 metre-long tapestry. This 19 metre section is approximately a quarter of the overall length.

www.mckinsey.com
A vertical scrollable time line which starts in the present. It is arranged in decades and provides more in-depth information for each decade. Depending on which year is activated, the appropriate information is shown in the visible section.

www.chicagostock-exchange.com
Presentation of the historical development of the stock exchange in Chicago. The time line is used as a navigation element to access the respective time sections.

Sept. 29, 1952
Trading hours change to 10 a.m. - 3:30 p.m. ET; no Saturdays.

Early 1960's
Midwest Stock Exchange Service Corporation is established to provide centralized accounting for member firms.

1959
New Orleans Stock Exchange becomes part of the Midwest Stock Exchange.

1955: Mayor Richard J. Daley elected

← Intro · · 1860 · · 1900 · · 1930 · · 1950 · · 1970 · · 1980 · · 1990 · · 1997 · · 2000 →

The Jerusalem
Archaeological Park

| ∷ Jerusalem Archaeological Park | ∷ Virtual Reconstruction Model | ∷ Davidson Center | · Biographies | · Timeline | · Bibliography |
| | | ∷ Park Map | · Historical Notes | · Glossary | · Historical Sources |

Home

Period	Events		Archaeological Remains
Umayyad period 660-750 CE	Extensive building by Caliph Adb al-Malik ibn al-Marwan and his son Al-Walid		The Dome of the Rock and the Al-Aqsa Mosque (on the Temple Mount), public buildings south of the Temple Mount
	749	Umayyad buildings, south of the Temple Mount destroyed in earthquake	
Abbasid and Fatimid period 750-1073 CE	1073	Jerusalem conquered by the Seljuks	

BCE	4500 - 1000	1000 - 586	538 - 70	70 - 325	325 - 634	660 - 1073	1099 - 1187	1187 - 1917	CE
	Pre First Temple period	First Temple period	Second Temple period	Roman period	Byzantine period	Early Islamic period	Crusader period	Late Islamic period	

www.archpark.org.il
Time line of the history of Jerusalem. Here, too, the time line is used as a navigation element which places the in-depth information in its historical context.

The zoom as a narrative framework

The zoom technique can be used to arrange information in a hierarchy from big to small or from the general to the specific in a continuous scale. Within the metaphor of the zoom, the information can be integrated in its context at the macro or micro level. The context is retained.

To move a step higher in the hierarchy the scale must be reduced, and to move a step lower in the hierarchy the scale must be increased. This navigation technique does not necessarily correspond to a "realistic" camera zoom – the decisive element is its plausibility.

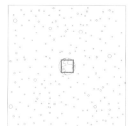

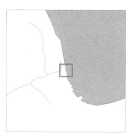
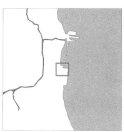

**isgwww.cs.uni-magdeburg
.de/~raab**
A distorted zoom is able to show a detail and its relative contextual position at the same time.

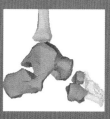
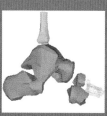

www.cs.sfu.ca
In addition to constant zooms, a number of different techniques have developed which distort by magnification and thus show a detail and its relative contextual position at the same time.

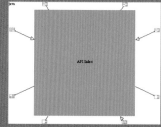
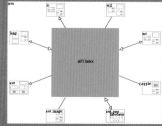
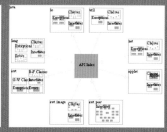

www.scanrail.com
This multimedia presentation for travelling through Scandinavia offers a zoomable map. With different layers additional information about the infrastructure can be added.

To increase the navigation convenience, a small overall view is often used. It shows the user's current position and the magnification scale. It also acts as a navigation instrument which enables the user to shift the viewing area at each level of the zoom.

Powers of ten
A film by the Eames office on the relative size of objects in the universe. A continuous zoom from outer space down to the atomic level places everything in a single context.

     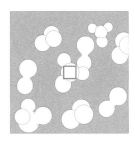

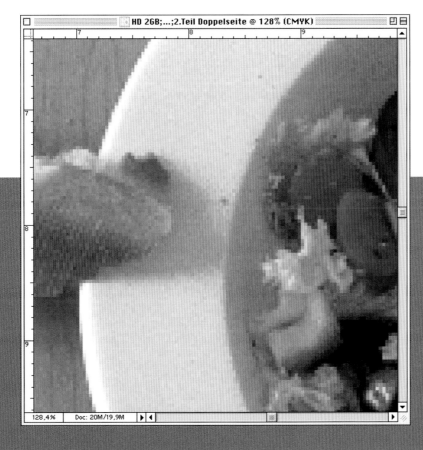

Adobe Photoshop 4.0 + >
The navigation window in this image-processing program enables the user to retouch individual pixels without losing the general overview.

www.nationalgeographic .com
This multimedia presentation of the attack on Pearl Harbor combines two navigation techniques, the time line and the zoom.

Computers are called computers because they can compute

The main feature of computers is their ability to carry out complex calculations and manage large amounts of data. The ability to organise this information by different criteria permits a flexible presentation of the information. In combination with the ability to carry out complex calculations, this means the end of lists, calculation formulae and tables. Tools are arising to replace complex calculations which were formerly carried out by specialists.

To make these tools as simple as possible, features are borrowed from the real world. Three-dimensional moving parts designate possibilities for interaction. This **illusion** helps to break down the fear of what is new and to minimise possible operating errors.

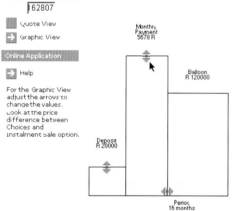

MacOS calculator
The classical desktop and pocket calculator in its abstracted form is an icon of a pocket calculator rather than a faithful representation.

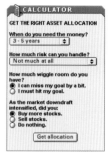

www.cnn.com/money
A calculation program to draw up a personal asset allocation.

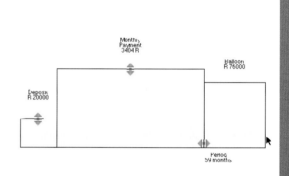

For the Graphic View adjust the arrows to change the values. Look at the price difference between Choices and Instalment Sale option.

www.daimler-chrysler.com
A calculation program to draw up financing plans.

AppleCDAudio
With this interface based on the appearance of a physical CD player, the operation of the software is immediately understandable.

www.cnn.com/money
"Moneyville" is a planning game for college leavers to determine the optimum finance plans.

Another area is the transfer of formerly analogue appliances to the digital world. The computer with multimedia capability enables sound and film sequences to be played, recorded and mixed. The necessary software is closely modelled on its real predecessors.

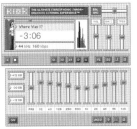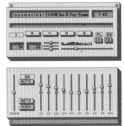

SoundJam
Different "skins" for a virtual sound desk.

see also pages 56|57

real media player

Apple Quicktime Player
The visual style of this software to play digital films seems to switch ironically between the hardware and the software. The surface seems to be made of polished stainless steel, but the window can be continuously and elastically increased or reduced in size.

www.eon.com
Tool on the site of an electricity supplier. The customer can put together the energy sources from which he wishes to receive electricity. The price and the CO_2 contamination level for this combination are then calculated directly.

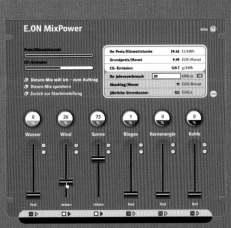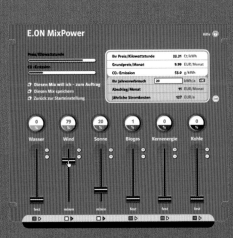

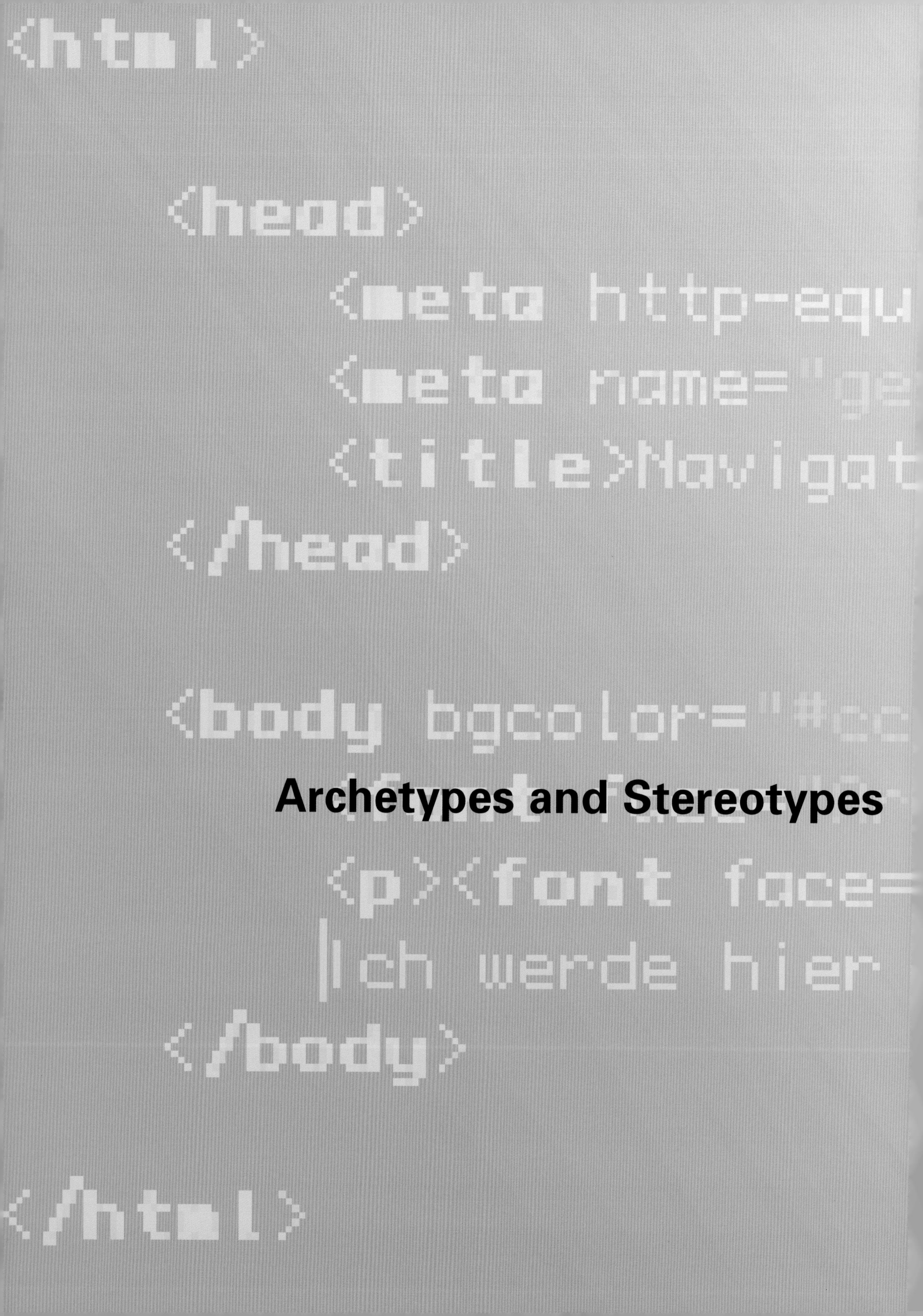

```
<html>

    <head

            <meta http-equ
            <meta name="ge
            <title>Navigat
        </head>


    <body bgcolor="#ee

            <p><font face=
        |ich werde hier
        </body>

</html>
```

Archetypes and Stereotypes

The Internet, or perhaps more precisely:
the **World Wide Web**, is about ten years old.
That means that it is time for a review. Have
codes, symbols or standards developed in
the global Web which can be understood in
an international setting? Is there a wealth of
different navigation techniques, or does the
necessity to be universally understood reduce
the possible forms of expression to the smallest
common denominator?

Have the technical requirements and
characteristics of the Internet created their
own separate aesthetics? Have media-specific
rituals and traditions started to develop?

Since the introduction of the first graphic browser, the Internet has developed into a field of activity for designers. The content is stored in the scripting language **HTML** and interpreted by an Internet browser. HTML is a page description language. A feature of this language is that the content and the formatting are stored separately.

This enables a cross-platform standard to be maintained. The content is stored together with formatting details in the form of **tags** and interpreted differently on different operating systems, **browsers** and monitors.

In addition, the user can change the display form for the pages. He or she can determine the font type and the display size, suppress pictures, or even ignore the layout details of the page and insist on display with **standard colours**.

HTML = Hypertext Markup Language.
The terms hypertext and hypermedia were created by Theodor Holm Nelson in the early 1960s. They involve creating connections between different content units by logical links to form a non-linear text.

Browse = glance through the pages in a leisurely way.
The first browser was developed by Tim Berners Lee in 1990. He also developed the part of the Internet which is known as the World Wide Web. The first graphical browser was called Mosaic and was developed by Marc Andreesen and Eric Bina in 1993.

Standard colours:

Background

Text

Link

Active Link

Visited Link

```
<html>

    <head>
        <meta http-equiv="content-type" content="text/html;charset=iso-8859-1">
        <meta name="generator" content="Adobe GoLive 4">
        <title>Navigation for the Internet and other Digital Media</title>
    </head>

    <body bgcolor="#cc3300" text="#ffffcc" link="white" alink="#ff6633" vlink="#cc9966">
        <font face="Arial,Helvetica,Geneva,Swiss,SunSans-Regular">So sieht eine einfache HTML-Seite aus, </fo
        <p><font face="Arial,Helvetica,Geneva,Swiss,SunSans-Regular">in der noch nicht viel drinsteht.
        Ich werde hier mal einen <a href="(Leere Referenz!)">Link</a> anlegen. </font>
    </body>

</html>
```

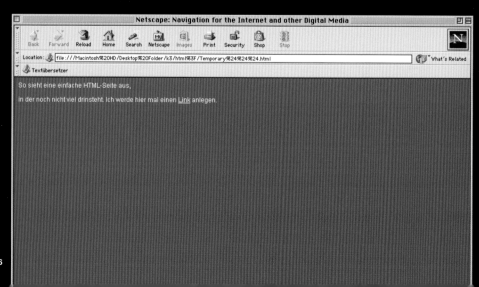

At the beginning of the 1990s, hypertext and its conventions had a dominant influence on the appearance of Web pages. Pictures in GIF format are integrated in the flow of the lines in the text. Links are coded by underlining. The prevailing concept is similar to the parchment roll: a long text that can be scrolled vertically. Different pages are linked by a simple menu at the top edge of the screen. Links offer cross-references to other text sections and pages. At the lower edge of the page there is a link "back to top of page" or a repetition of the menu.

This feature irritates many designers who have a traditional, static concept of design. The difference between classical graphic design and Web design can be compared with the difference between bitmap graphics and vector graphics. In one case the result is a finished layout, in the other case only a guideline is provided which leaves scope for interpretation in the implementation.

www.kah-bonn.de
Website of the art and exhibition hall of the Federal Republic of Germany in Bonn. This site uses the dynamic line break as a design element.

www.dunvagen.com
Website of the musician Philip Glass shows different line breaks and dynamic adjustment of image size as a result of three different browser settings.

"Inventions then cannot, in nature, be a subject of property."
Thomas Jefferson

For navigation, an initial feature quickly became more or less standard: the **menu** as a marginal column at the left of the window. This principle still survives today in innumerable variations, and it has proved to be rather efficient. The HTML standard developed further, and the introduction of **frames** which can be accessed in different ways enabled two hierarchical levels to be displayed at the same time. This saves the "reverse gear" in navigation. It is possible to move backwards and forwards between different pages within the same hierarchical level. The "Back" and "Home" links are superfluous. In addition, the main menu in the margin column can be extended by extra sub-menus. For layouts that are loaded as whole pages, this navigation structure has also become a reliable and widespread navigation standard which can be quickly grasped.

Menu = a choice of items from a list.
The points are similar to the selection on a restaurant menu.

Frames: in this technique, several HTML pages are loaded into an HTML document which defines frames. This enables parts of the area within the window to be replaced separately.

www.blaxxun.com
The main menu can be extended by two more drop-down sub-menus.

www.apple.com
The main menu, and the
second hierarchical level
are designed as three-
dimensional index tabs.

www.form.de
The same principle as on
the Apple website, but
here in a purely graphical
design.

Parallel to the development of the vertical
menu, the horizontal menu at the upper or
lower edge of the image also developed.
The horizontal menu at the top edge often
uses an index tab analogy, which is used in
many programs and was originally borrowed
from office filing systems.
A horizontal menu is useful if the number of
menu items is relatively small. This menu
principle is now established, so that even
menus of two or three lines at the top edge
of the image are understandable, although
linking the menus with the content is a more
difficult design task.

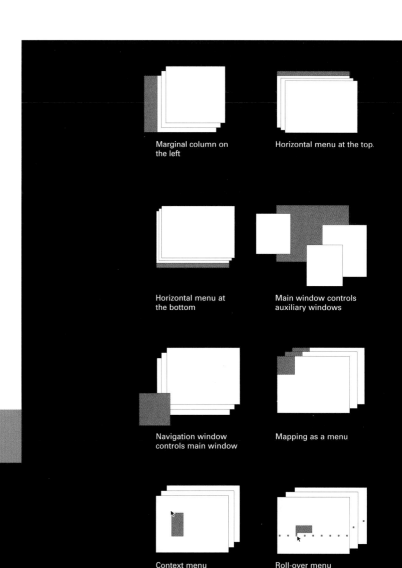

Marginal column on
the left

Horizontal menu at the top

Horizontal menu at
the bottom

Main window controls
auxiliary windows

Navigation window
controls main window

Mapping as a menu

Context menu

Roll-over menu

Menu bars on the bottom edge of the image are standard for kiosk applications with a touchscreen. They are increasingly popular in Internet applications and form a design alternative to the horizontal menu at the top edge of the window.

Fixed window proportions, such as those in **Flash** applications, guarantee permanent visibility of the menu options.

Flash is a vector-based animation program.

As in application programs, concepts have become established to distribute the content over several windows. This means that loading times can be used more efficiently.

The basic information in the main window is loaded quickly, and each user can supplement it with image and graphic material as he or she wishes; this then opens a separate window of a size adapted to the content.

www.jeepunpaved.com
Extract from the site of the American motor company Jeep. Tabs at the lower edge of the window extend and offer the associated sub-menus.

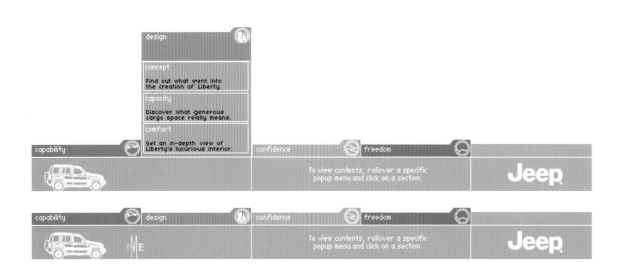

*Actual figure in the autumn of 2000: 407 million users

An extra window can also be opened for navigation purposes by offering a site map which is left permanently open for better orientation.

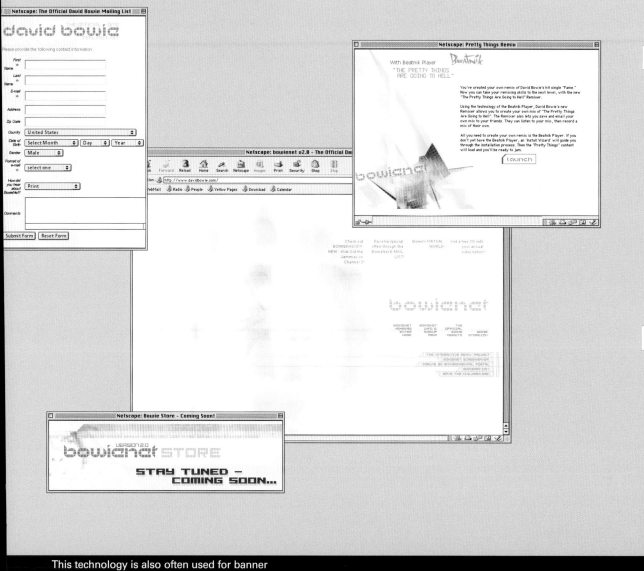

www.davidbowie.com
The website of the musician David Bowie. A separate window is opened for each category.

www.DKNY.com
The main window contains three menu items, each of which opens a separate window.

This technology is also often used for banner advertising. There it has the advantage that the window initially has a high attention value, but can then be closed to free valuable space on the monitor.

The screen is always too small

UPDATES
NETWORK
REFERENCES
JOBS
FREESTYLE
CONTACT
X

UPDATES
NETWORK
REFERENCES
JOBS
FREESTYLE
CONTACT
X

www.nasa20.com
The main menu is
represented by a square
that follows the cursor and
unfolds on roll-over.

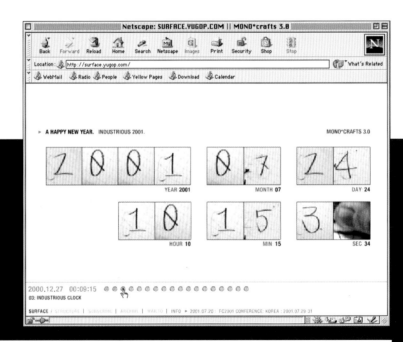

www.yugop.com
The main menu appears
as a status bar at the lower
edge of the image and
changes colour gradually
to adjust to the respective
content page.

Netscape: SURFACE.YUGOP.COM || MONO*crafts 3.0

Location: http://surface.yugop.com/   What's Related

WebMail   Radio   People   Yellow Pages   Download   Calendar

▸ **A HAPPY NEW YEAR.** INDUSTRIOUS 2001.   MONO*CRAFTS 3.0

YEAR **2001**   MONTH **07**   DAY **24**

HOUR **10**   MIN **15**   SEC **34**

2000.12.27 00:09:15
03: INDUSTRIOUS CLOCK

SURFACE / STRUCTURE | SUBSCRIBE | ARCHIVE | MAILTO | INFO ▸ 2001.07.20 : FC2001 CONFERENCE: KOREA : 2001.07.29-31

2000.12.27 00:09:15
03: INDUSTRIOUS CLOCK

SURFACE / STRUCTURE | SUBSCRIBE | ARCHIVE | MAILTO | INFO ▸ 2001.07.20 : FC2001 CONFERENCE: KOREA : 2001.07.29-31

2001.01.20 00:49:15
05: FINGERTRACKS : STUDY-A

SURFACE / STRUCTURE | SUBSCRIBE | ARCHIVE | MAILTO | INFO   2001.05.14 : IdN FRESHCONFERENCE : SYDNEY : 2001.09.28-29

2001.07.09 03:06:05
18: RIGID BODY 02

SURFACE / STRUCTURE | SUBSCRIBE | ARCHIVE | MAILTO | INFO ▸ 2001.07.20 : FC2001 CONFERENCE: KOREA : 2001.07.29-31

2001.05.19 00:18:20
16: LINE X 50

Methods have developed for all types of menus to occupy screen space only temporarily. Pull-down menus and pop-up menus are already known from application programs in the world of computers. They are extended by many more variations in the Internet due to the shorter cycle of innovation on the Web.

Roll-over menus and context menus reduce the visual complexity and minimise the space needed for control elements.

www.apple.com
In the sub-menu for technical support, additional sub-menus are shown by roll-over.

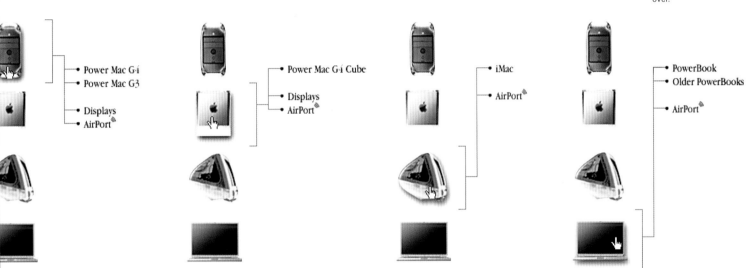

www.porches.com
Roll-over dynamically adds sub-menus to the main menu.

"Thus, in the 20th century, we have been without any mass medium for serious discourse – until the creation of the Internet."

Alan Kay

www.focus.de
The site map of a German news magazine with a scroll list which marks the hierarchical levels by using indentation and colour.

www.lycos.com
The site map of the Internet portal Lycos is a scrollable tableau of all areas. The link lists are blue and underlined in keeping with the Internet convention.

Lycos Site Map

Personalize
- Build A Website
- Calendar
- Horoscopes
- Lycos Browser
- My Investing
- My Lycos
- News & Gossip
- More

Communicate
- Build a Home Page
- Chat
- Clubs
- Email
- Finance Seminars
- Image Galleries
- Instant Messaging
- Message Boards
- Mobile Access & Services
- Newsgroups
- Relationships
- Video

Shop
DEPARTMENTS
- Autos
- Babies & Toddlers
- Books
- Business Services
- Cell Phones
- Clothing
- Computers
- Electronics
- Gifts & Flowers
- More

SERVICES
- Lycos Mastercard
- Lycos Rewards Program
- Lycos Shipping Center
- Lycos Wireless Marketplace

AUCTIONS
- Arts & Antiques
- Coins & Stamps
- Collectibles
- More

CLASSIFIEDS
- Autos
- Careers
- Real Estate
- More

MERCHANT MATCH
- Home Services
- Travel & Lodging
- Real Estate

Lycos Network
- Angelfire.com
- Gamesville.com
- HTMLgear.com
- Hotbot.com
- Hotwired.com
- Lycos.com
- Matchmaker.com
- Quote.com
- RagingBull.com
- Sonique.com
- Tripod.com
- Wired.com
- Webmonkey.com
- WhoWhere.com

Topics on Lycos

Arts
- Literature
- Photography
- Visual Arts
- Website Directory
- More

Autos
- Buy
- Research
- Sell
- Website Directory
- More

Careers
- Company Profiles
- Job Search
- Resumes
- Website Directory
- More

College
- Academic Issues
- Greek Life
- Roommates & Housing
- Website Directory
- More

Computers
- Downloads
- Hardware Reviews
- Help & How-To
- Website Directory
- More

Entertainment
- Celebrities
- Pictures
- TV
- Website Directory
- More

Finance
- Markets
- Live Charts
- Trading
- Website Directory
- More

Games
- Cards
- Classic
- Lottery
- Website Directory
- More

Regional
- Asia
- Europe
- U.S.
- Website Directory
- More

Health
- Conditions A-Z
- Medical Library
- News
- Website Directory
- More

Home & Family
- Gardens
- Pets
- Recipes
- Website Directory
- More

Kids
- FunZone
- Games
- Homework
- Website Directory
- More

Music
- Concert Listings
- Downloads
- Free MP3s & Player
- Website Directory
- More

Real Estate
- Buy
- Sell
- Finance
- Website Directory
- More

Reference
- Databases
- Education
- Maps
- Website Directory
- More

Relationships
- Dating
- Personals
- Romance
- More

Science & Technology
- Physics
- Environment
- Astronomy
- Website Directory
- More

Small Business
- Business-to-Business
- News
- Tools
- Website Directory
- More

Society & Beliefs
- Genealogy
- Romance
- Women
- Website Directory
- More

Sports
- Baseball
- NFL
- NCAA Football
- Fantasy
- Website Directory
- More

Travel
- Book Flights
- Cruises
- Hotel Reservations
- Vacations Packages
- Website Directory
- More

Website Building
- Build A Home Page
- Tools
- Tutorials
- Website Directory
- More

Search the Web
- Advanced Search
- Hotbot Search
- Lycos Search

ALSO
- Add Your Site To Lycos
- Parental Controls

Find
- Auctions
- Books
- Classifieds
- Concert Listings
- Dictionary
- Downloads Reviewed
- Email Addresses
- Files (FTP)
- Job Listings
- Lottery
- Maps & Driving Directions
- Music (MP3s)
- News Articles
- Personal Home Pages
- Pictures/Graphics
- Movies/Video
- Sounds/Audio
- Shipping
- Shopping
- Stock Quotes
- TV Listings
- Weather Forecasts
- White Pages
- Yellow Pages

Tools
- Home Page Builder
- HTMLgear For Your Site
- Lycos Browser
- Lycos Mobile
- Parental Controls
- Personalize Lycos
- QCharts-Trading Application
- Sonique MP3 player

About Lycos
LEARN ABOUT US
- Corporate Information
- Press Releases
- See The Help section

CONTACT US
- Add Your Site To Lycos
- Advertise On Lycos
- Jobs At Lycos
- Join Our Affiliate program
- Send Us Feedback

Lycos Worldwide
Europe: Austria, Belgium, Denmark, France, Germany, Italy, Netherlands, Norway, Spain, Sweden, Switzerland, UK
Asia Pacific: China, Hong Kong, India, Indonesia, Japan, Korea, Malaysia, Philippines, Singapore, Southeast Asia, Taiwan, Thailand
Americas: Argentina, Brazil, Canada, Caribbean, Chile, Colombia, Estados Unidos, Mexico, Peru, Venezuela

www.wilkhahn.com
The site map of a German furniture manufacturer. A building plan is shown on a slide which shows the different areas of the site.

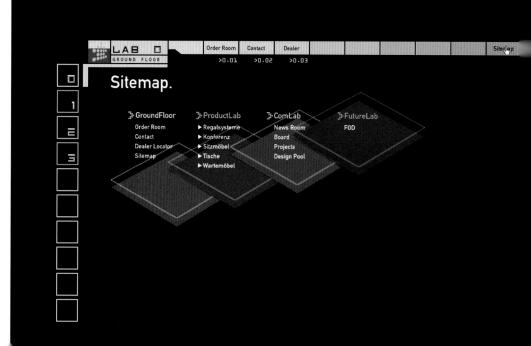

Site maps are a classical aspect of most websites. They provide a general overview, give an indication of the size of a site and help the user to find specific information. In the early period of the World Wide Web there was often an illustrative and literal interpretation of the map, i.e. a "geographical" map of the site. This form is now increasingly replaced by a list sorted by categories. This is probably for practical reasons because a mental model, even if it is only an organisational diagram of a site, is more difficult to extend. From a certain level of complexity, the clarity of the structure also suffers. However, an illustration is easier to remember than a text list.

The more interactive Web applications become, the less important page-based thinking becomes. This means that the content can no longer be shown by breaking it down into individual pages. **Mental models** which help the user to find and recover information still remain important navigation aids.

see also pages 116|117

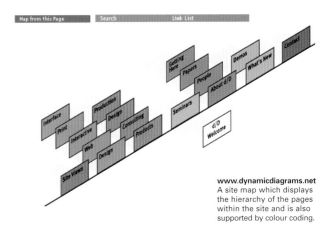

www.dynamicdiagrams.net
A site map which displays the hierarchy of the pages within the site and is also supported by colour coding.

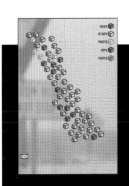
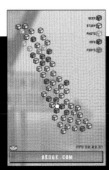
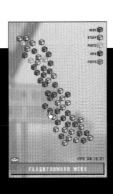
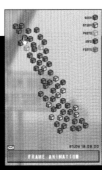

www.natzke.com
The site map of an experimental website which accommodates various artists. The site map itself is used here as a navigation tool. The areas that have already been visited are marked in colour so that the visitor can easily recognise which areas he or she has already seen.

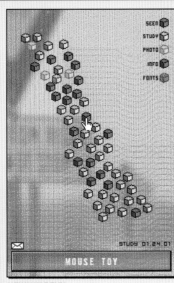

Buttons

How do I explain to a user when he or she must be active? Graphical interfaces start with what is familiar and offer three-dimensional illustrations to mark interaction areas, and thus to visualise the associated functions. In keeping with the standard practice in computer applications, tools and control elements are borrowed from the real world.

But we can see that the mere imitation of keys is gradually disappearing. A variety of possible and impossible mechanisms is arising which are abstract or hyper-realistic in appearance and no longer correspond to anything in the real world.

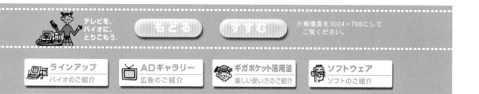

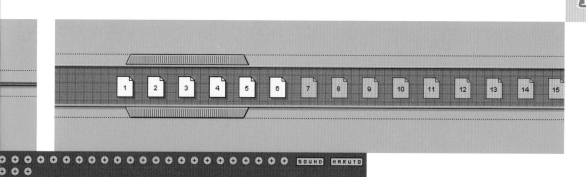

EMAIL

Magnifier ▲ ▲▲ ✕

GO!

Hot News Headlines   Jobs Previews Next Version of Mac OS X and iDVD 2.

MILKO MUSIC MACHINE™   **START**

Search

Metal   Hip-hop   Disco

◆ SEND   ◆ PRINT   ◆ INFO   ◆ HELP

RULES   WINNERS

TOOLS   SPEED   START STOP   CLEAR

▦ Jerusalem   • Virtual   ▪ Davidson Center   • Biographies   • Timeline   • Bibliography
Archaeological Park   Reconstruction Model   ▦ Park Map   • Historical Notes   • Glossary   Historical Sources

DONE VOTING

BCE	4500 - 1000	1000 - 586	538 - 70	70 - 325	325 - 634	660 - 1073	1099 - 1187	1187 - 1917	CE
	Pre First Temple period	First Temple period	Second Temple period	Roman period	Byzantine period	Early Islamic period	Crusader period	Late Islamic period	

POPUP

NORMAL

FULLSCREEN

Design options are continually expanding by
integrating or accessing other scripts.
In addition to CSS, JavaScript and Java,
there is also DHTML. The fact that the source
code of each page can be made visible leads
to a dynamic development, especially in
JavaScript scripts.

Higher transmission rates and vector-based
animation techniques are making Internet
applications more interactive. The passive
reading approach is being broken down by
integrating the user. As a result, Internet
applications are achieving an interaction
culture which was once only offered by
off-line applications.

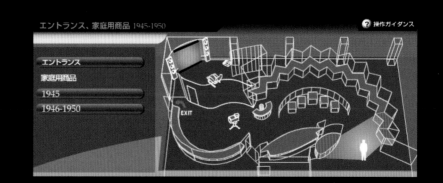

エントランス、家庭用商品 1945-1950   ❓ 操作ガイダンス

エントランス

家庭用商品

1945

1946-1950

EXIT

see also pages 32|33

LOADING
73%

LOADING

Feedback plays a central role in interactive systems. This applies especially to the Internet where unstable connections, slow loading times and corrupted scripts can lead to delays and computer crashes. All indications that the system is still working and the activities of the user are registered have the effect of creating confidence.

The animated logo of the browser is not just decorative, it is a sign of life.

Slow loading times for sites with a heavy emphasis on pictures are still unavoidable, in fact, transmission rates and sites are engaged in a sort of race. The faster the transmission rates, the larger websites become. To bridge this loading time and give the user information about the size of the site being loaded and the approximate time needed, "loading" sequences have become more or less standard.

Street

Gifts

Hair

L oADIN G

Loading.

Loading..

Loading...

LOADING MIES IN BERLIN

LOADING MIES VAN DER ROHE DATA

LOADING

LOADING

LOADING

0 25 5 75 1

(The Eneri Prayer)   (The Eneri Prayer)   (The Eneri Praye

LOADING 220K...   LOADING 220K...   LOADING 22

loading...

pardon the delay, loading 110k

Loading Game...

LOADING STANCE .   LOADING STANCE .

NOW LOADING   PLEASE WAIT.

LOADING...

Loading.

<<<   LOADING   >>>

LOADING 70K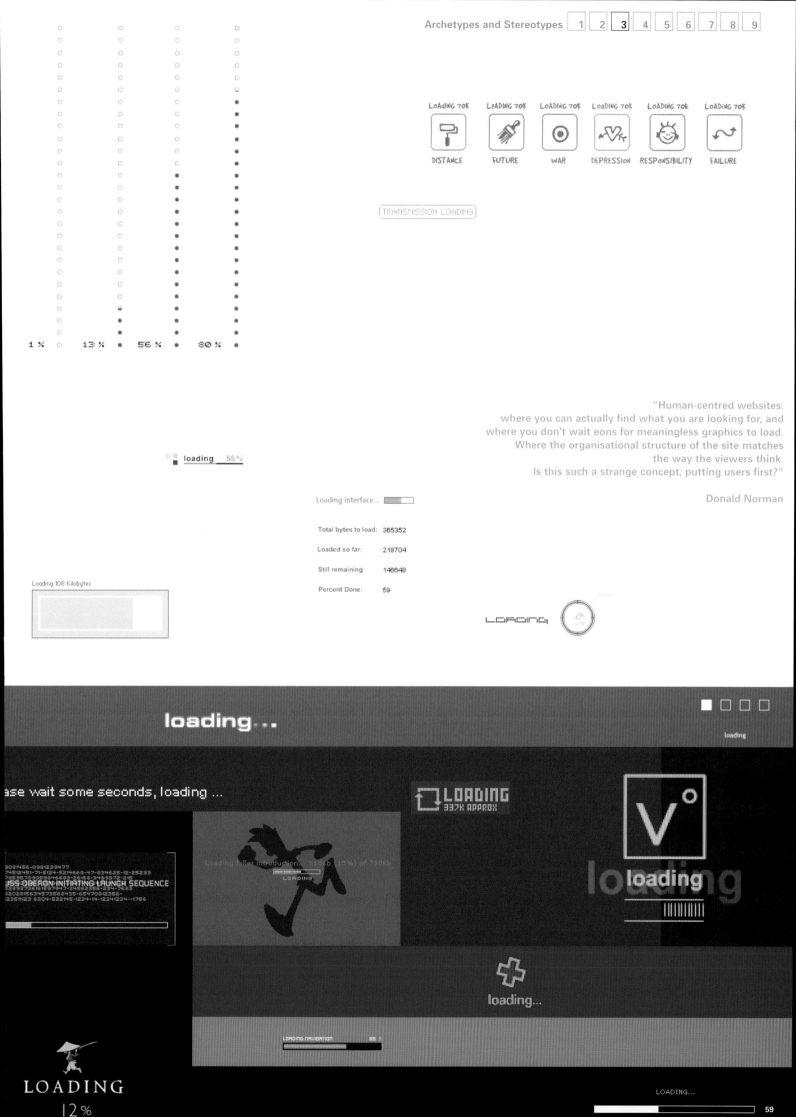
DISTANCE

LOADING 70K
FUTURE

LOADING 70K
WAR

LOADING 70K
DEPRESSION

LOADING 70K
RESPONSIBILITY

LOADING 70K
FAILURE

TRANSMISSION LOADING

1 %   13 %   56 %   80 %

"Human-centred websites:
where you can actually find what you are looking for, and
where you don't wait eons for meaningless graphics to load.
Where the organisational structure of the site matches
the way the viewers think.
Is this such a strange concept; putting users first?"

Donald Norman

loading   55%

Loading interface...

Total bytes to load: 365352

Loaded so far: 218704

Still remaining: 146648

Percent Done: 59

Loading 108 Kilobytes

LOADING

loading...

loading

ase wait some seconds, loading ...

LOADING
332K APPROX

V°
loading

USS OBERON: INITIATING LAUNCH SEQUENCE

LOADING

loading...

LOADING:NAVIGATION   65 %

LOADING
12 %

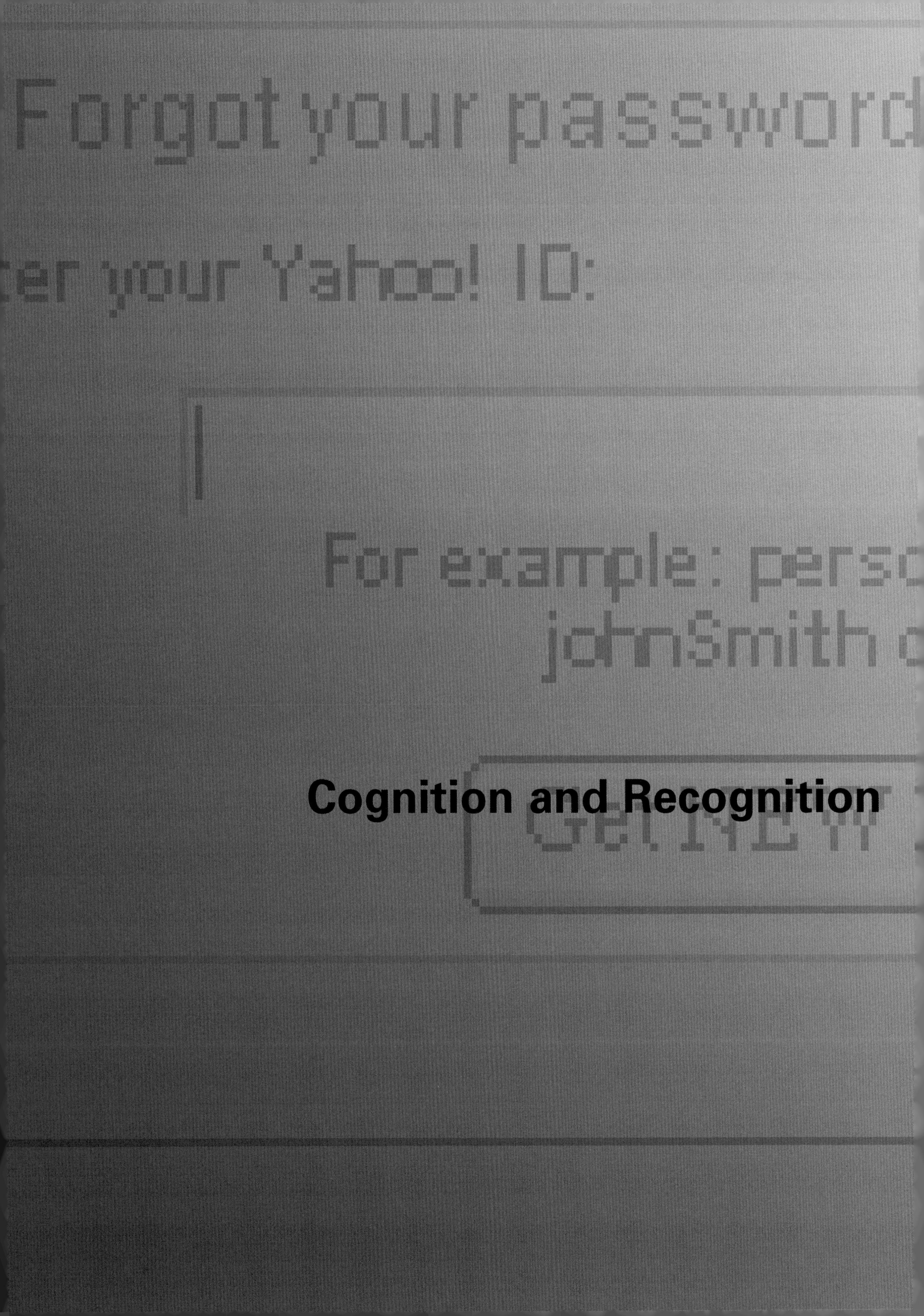

Forgot your password

ter your Yahoo! ID:

For example: persc
johnSmith c

Cognition and Recognition

1   2   3   **4**   5   6   7   8   9

How does a visitor experience a website when he visits it for the first time?
Can a visitor find his way around at once?
Are there traffic signs and signposts on the Web?
To enable us to grasp complex information more quickly, visualisation is an important feature. The medium can extend traditional information processing by adding the dimensions of time and interaction.
Visual, synchronous optical processing of data in real-time is the next challenge for the Internet. This chapter shows websites that already work on this principle.

You never get a second chance to make a first impression

The home page is what the visitor sees first after he or she has entered the **URL**. It is the first contact between the visitor and the site, unless there is a prior introduction to welcome the user. The first visit to a website is similar to entering a room – it conveys a lot of information. Some of this information is received directly and some is perceived in the atmosphere, i.e. largely subconsciously. The colours, symbols and images used, which depend on the content and orientation of the website, and the typographical design visualise the theme of the website in a number of ways.

Uniform Resource Locator
= Internet address.

The task and challenge for the designer is to take into account the specific features of the medium, such as the screen resolution and transmission rate, and to use images and graphic elements which are original and at the same time recognisable as symbols.

If there is a corporate identity concept for classical communication, this must be interpreted in a way that is appropriate for the medium. It can frequently be seen that the designers have not yet turned away from traditional communication media. The white background which is often used is usually an unquestioned relic from print media. The natural condition of paper is white, but the natural condition of a screen is black.

www.yahoo.com
First visit to the website of
the on-line portal Yahoo.

---

www.deutschebank.de
First visit to the website
of the German bank of
that name.

"You cannot not communicate."
Erik Spiekermann

Second visit.

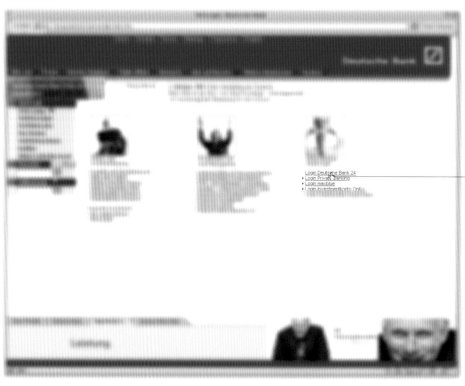

Sites which make copious use of colour: Optimum legibility is achieved here by carefully using brightness and colour contrast.

The contrast of brightness achieved by using black type on a white background or white type on a black background leads to blooming and flickering on the screen.

www.fitch.com   www.lhw.com   www.sony.com   www.abc.com   www.premiereworld.de

Second visit.

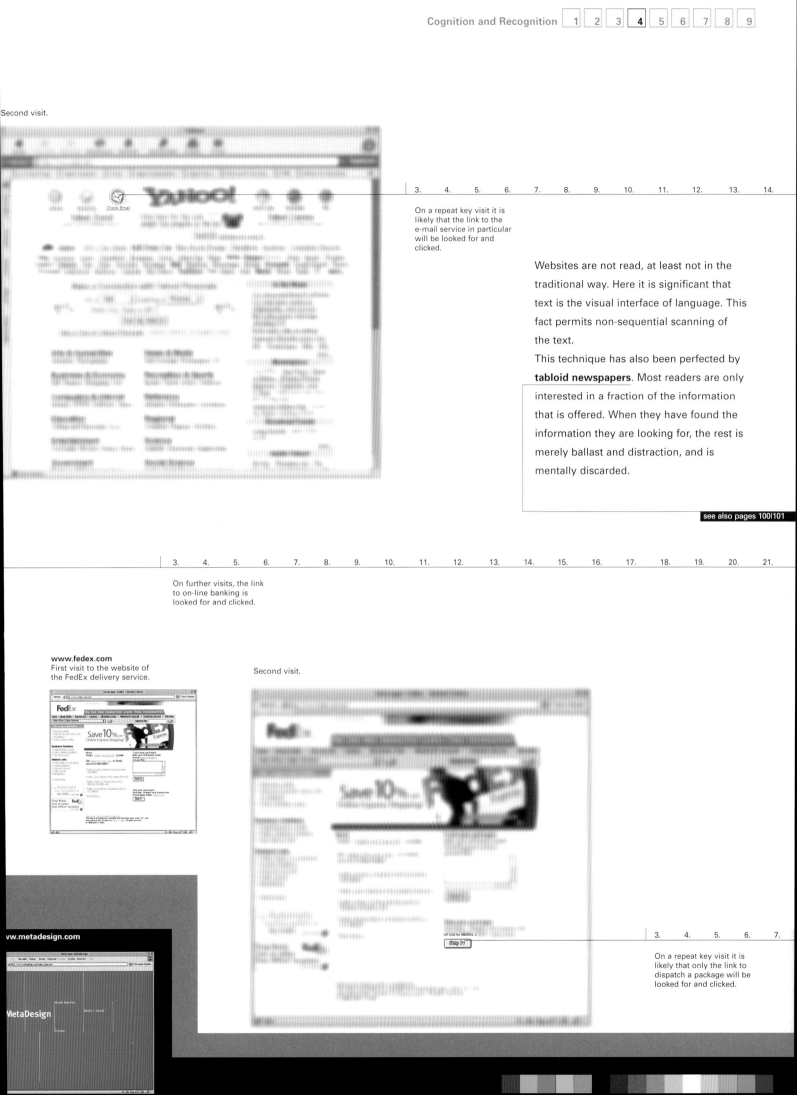

3.   4.   5.   6.   7.   8.   9.   10.   11.   12.   13.   14.

On a repeat key visit it is likely that the link to the e-mail service in particular will be looked for and clicked.

Websites are not read, at least not in the traditional way. Here it is significant that text is the visual interface of language. This fact permits non-sequential scanning of the text.

This technique has also been perfected by **tabloid newspapers**. Most readers are only interested in a fraction of the information that is offered. When they have found the information they are looking for, the rest is merely ballast and distraction, and is mentally discarded.

see also pages 100|101

3.   4.   5.   6.   7.   8.   9.   10.   11.   12.   13.   14.   15.   16.   17.   18.   19.   20.   21.

On further visits, the link to on-line banking is looked for and clicked.

www.fedex.com
First visit to the website of the FedEx delivery service.

Second visit.

vw.metadesign.com

MetaDesign

3.   4.   5.   6.   7.

On a repeat key visit it is likely that only the link to dispatch a package will be looked for and clicked.

Symbols: signposts, instructions and short stories

Visual communication with the aid of symbols has a long tradition. The alphabets originally developed as a result of an abstraction of picture symbols. The use of **pictograms** today represents a communication technique which crosses language barriers.

The symbols not only depict an object, they also contain an instruction for action. The pictogram showing an umbrella does not mean the umbrella itself, but that the object which is marked with the symbol must be protected from moisture.

This cave painting from the mesolithic age comes from the Vallorta gorge in eastern Spain.
The visualised story can still be understood today.

Common international pictograms. They are sometimes ambiguous, for example the symbols for lifts and toilets are sometimes confused.

Symbols of the Japanese samurai, whose culture developed for seven centuries from the tenth century onwards.

see | tiny | female person | deity | fabric | male person | child | water | wooden item | plant | tree | walk

path | fire | snake | house | town | stone | sun | mountain

Hieroglyphs are remarkably stable in their form even over millennia. The symbols of the Egyptians (about 3000 B.C.) are almost directly understandable, but the abstract symbols of the Maya (1000 B.C.) leave more scope for interpretation.

Kwikpoint. A non-verbal picture lexicon which can be understood internationally.

Some symbols are not immediately understandable, they must be learned. But when they have been learned, they allow faster access to information. Symbols can be charged with different meanings as is shown, for example, by the emblems of major companies. They contain a cloud of meanings which comprise and communicate the company itself, its field of business and its qualities. These symbols thus become signposts on the Internet.

Instructions in comic form, in this case a Chinese cooking recipe.

Brand emblems as signposts on the Web. Where it is not possible to check the quality of goods and services personally, this is made up for by confidence in a brand name.

Pattern recognition

The human memory works particularly well with visual pattern recognition. We can recognise what we have seen previously, even if we see it in a changed form. This ability seems particularly strong in the recognition of human faces. We still recognise people, even if we haven't seen them for years and they have drastically changed their appearance.

The representation of image files by thumbnails is a successful use of this mnemonic pattern recognition principle. Thumbnails are automatically generated pictograms of the images they represent. Although they are greatly reduced in size and the image itself is usually not clearly recognisable, the distribution of contrast and colour is sufficient to recognise a previously seen image.

Thumbnails are a valuable help to our memory in recovering information. Created here by the program Adobe Photoshop.

see also pages 98|99

"Words and language, whether written or spoken, do not seem to play any role at all in the mechanism of my thought processes. The basic psychological elements of thought are certain symbols and more or less clear images which can be reproduced or combined 'at will'."

Albert Einstein

This principle works not only for images, but also for text files. **E-paper** applications such as Adobe Acrobat use page miniatures for navigation. Thus, a pictogram is generated for each page, and this facilitates fast navigation within large quantities of text.

Thumbnails of text pages as an aid to navigation in large quantities of text, here miniatures in Adobe Acrobat.

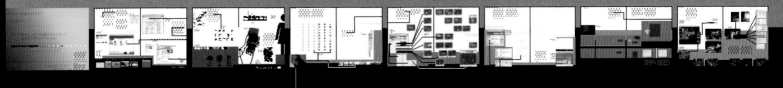

Visualisation of information: the map

The preservation of geographical facts in the form of a **map** has a long tradition. The possibility of gaining a general overview in this way makes them an important navigation tool. A further advantage is that other information can be presented on a geographical map. Maps are an organisational criterion by which data can be sorted, arranged and shown in a context.

Web-based applications can update this data frequently and compile it as the user requires. The more often the user has looked at a map, the quicker he will be able to pick out the required information.

see also pages 14|15

US Soil Moisture

US Respiratory Index

US Weather Today

www.weather.com
A website which provides weather forecasts processed in different ways depending on the needs and the situation.

US 24 Hour Temperature Change

The different maps are combined in different ways, depending on the category selected.

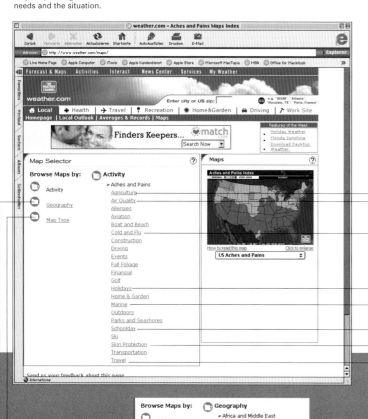

US Aches and Pains

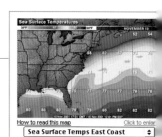

Sea Surface Temps East Coast

Schoolday Weather

Browse Maps by: **Geography**
‣ Africa and Middle East
Alaska US
Asia
Australia
Central America
Central US
East Central US
Europe
Hawaii US
Midwest US
North America
North Central US
Northeast US
Northwest US
Oceans
Pacific
Polar
South America
South Central US
Southeast US
Southwest US
US National Current
US National Forecast
US National Severe

Browse Maps by: **Map Type**
‣ Current Weather US National
Current Weather US Regional
Doppler Radar US
Earthquake Reports
Forecasts US National
Forecasts US Regional
Satellite US National
Satellite World
Severe US National
Severe US Regional
Ten Day Forecast US National

US Drought Severity

US Planting-Early June

US Precipitation Forecast

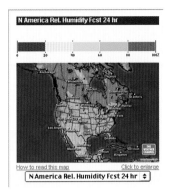

N America Rel. Humidity Fcst 24 hr

US Actual High Temps

US Actual Low Temps

US Current Dew Points

US Forecast Winds

Probability of a White Christmas

US 90 Day Temperature

"Throughout history, maps have always been equated with power, whether they depicted hunting grounds, trade routes, military sites, or buried treasure."

Richard Saul Wurman

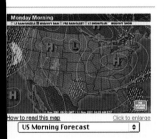

US Morning Forecast

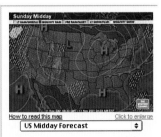

US Midday Forecast

US Energy Consumption Today

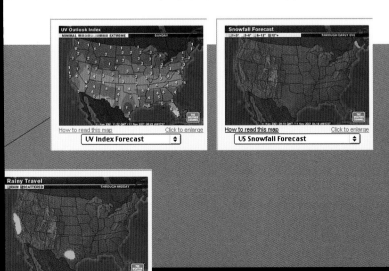

UV Index Forecast

US Snowfall Forecast

US Rainy Travel Now

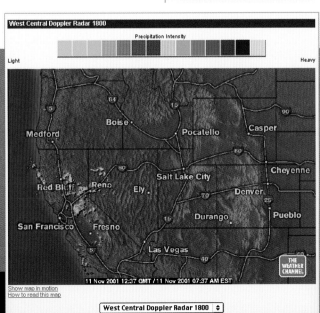

West Central Doppler Radar 1800

Mapping Information

The heavy emphasis on text on the Internet, which arose for technical reasons, is declining. In addition to the poor legibility of text on the screen, **absorbing information** in text form is a comparatively slow process. The use of visual resources is more appropriate for the medium and better as a means of communication. The medium is increasingly able to present multimedia information at acceptable speeds.

www.sfmoma.org
On-line discussion forum on the website of the Museum of Modern Art in San Francisco.

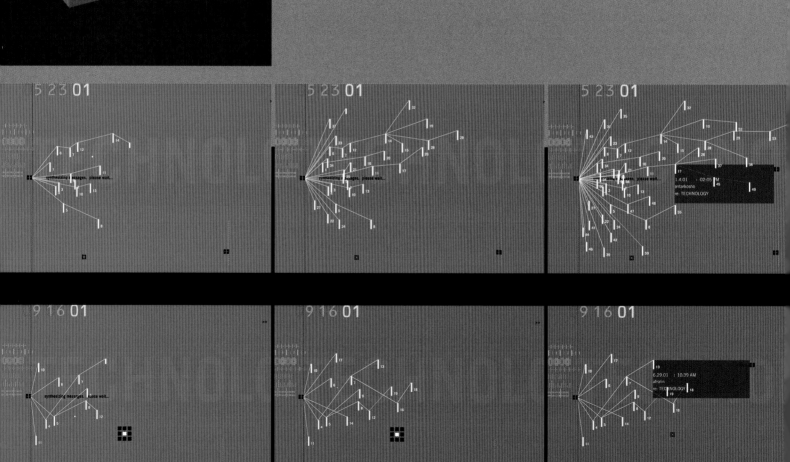

Our visual perception can process different sensory impressions received by the eye concurrently. This enables us, for example, to drive a car through road traffic. The sensory processing speed can be improved by training – and people in the 21st century have certainly developed it further than ever before.

On the Web, this ability can be used to grasp complex subject matter quickly. To facilitate this, the information must be presented in graphic form so that the user can quickly gain a general overview. The user must then be able to call up detailed information in a logical and plausible manner. For clear navigation, it is important that the user should never lose sight of the overall whole.

see also pages 98|99

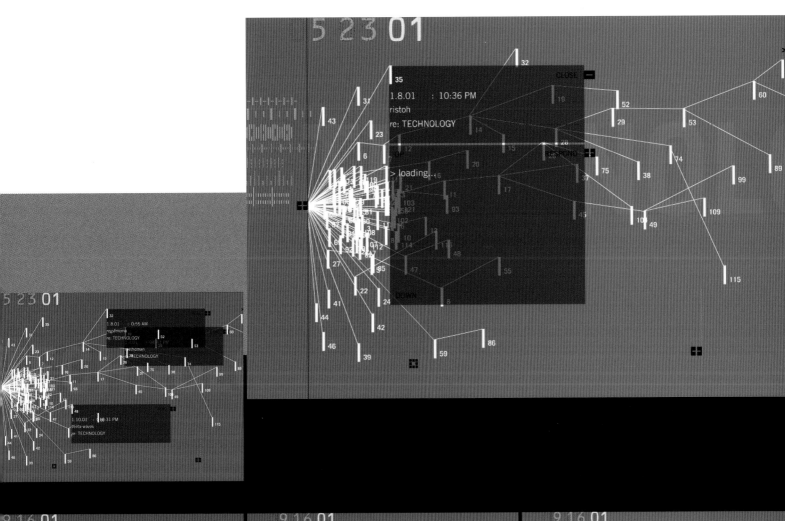

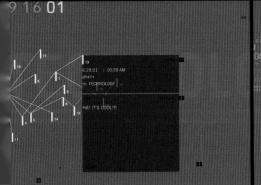

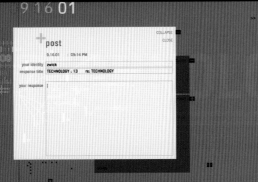

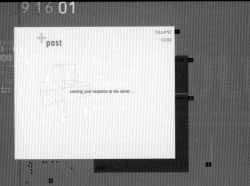

Mapping Information

The medium is able to cross-index information visually: the user can sort the data by different criteria, combine data and thus consider the information from different perspectives. He can also select and change the degree of complexity. In addition to the parameters of size, colour and position, in the digital medium it is possible to use speed and behaviour to code information.

www.smartmoney.com
A website which visualises stock market data in a mapping structure. This presentation provides an immediate overview of the present state of the market; more detailed information can be called up when necessary.

Small deviations in the performance of individual shares can be seen immediately by the different colour shades.

Stock market news can be called up in the mapping presentation.

The colour scale for the display of values can be adapted to the user's requirements.

27.9.2001

8.10.2001

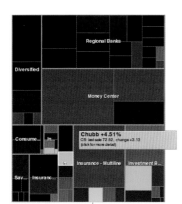

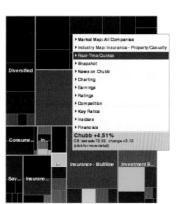

More detailed information about a company can be arranged by different criteria and called up immediately.

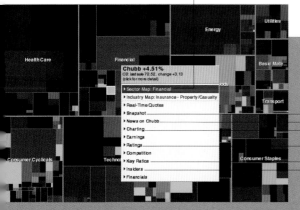

The synchronous optical presentation enables the eye to perceive even minimal differences and deviations, whereas only greater differences can be recognised by using the memory. These advantages of visual perception should be exploited to convert raw data into useful information – as is illustrated by the extremely successful example of a site which processes stock market data in map form.

This presentation permits a maximum speed of access to the current stock market data. A quick glance is all that is needed to grasp the "mood" of the market. After a short learning phase, the condition of individual sectors of the economy can be interpreted like a weather map. Where needed, more detailed information about individual companies can be called up at any point.

10.10.2001   15.10.2001   18.10.2001

Dynamic visualisation of information

To provide up-to-date and individually compiled information, it is necessary to visualise the data dynamically, i.e. at the moment of the query.

Internet applications which visualise data dynamically, e.g. calculating and displaying individual travel routes, are increasingly complex in their planning and programing. As a result, the work on the implementation of such applications is increasingly shared in a team.

The designer works out the concept and creates the visualisation by an informative simulation. The implementation then demands a specialist with knowledge of higher programing languages. But here, too, tools and applications are developed which permit, for example, the implementation of associative databases based on visual representation.

"Recognition is finding things. I am always delighted when I suggest an idea to someone, and they say, 'That is obvious. I could have thought of that'. That means that they have seen how one idea is connected to another."

Richard Saul Wurman

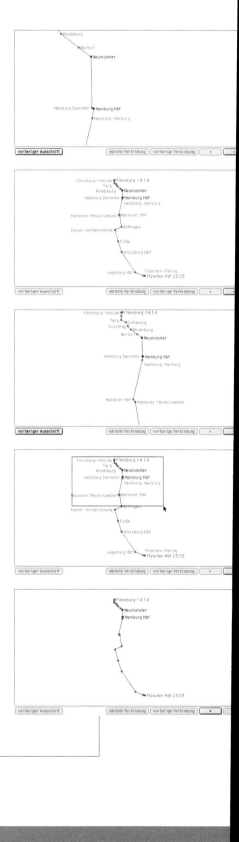

www.deutschebahn.de
The website of the German railway company. Timetable information can be obtained optionally as a table or a graphic.

First the starting point and destination are entered, then the route for the journey and all intermediate stops are generated as a zoomable image.

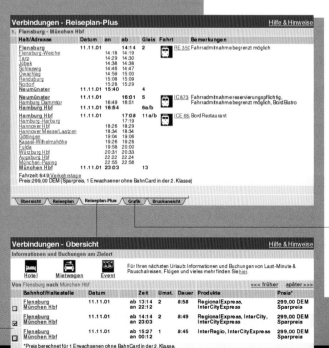

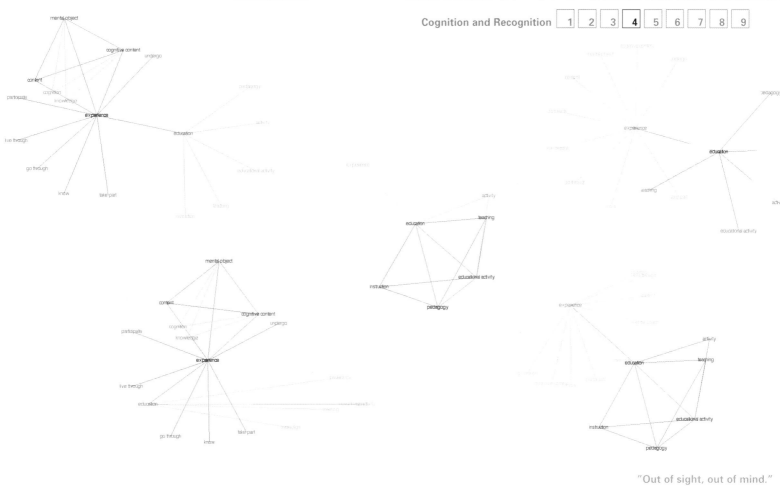

"Out of sight, out of mind."
Folk saying

www.plumbdesign.com
A website which has specialised in the visualisation of data, here the application of a visual thesaurus.

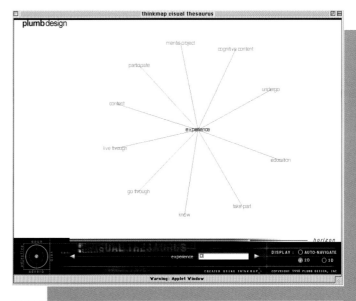

www.thinkmap.com
A software program that can be used to create visual databases. Links between the parameters to be portrayed and their visual representation open up new possibilities, but also create a new degree of complexity.

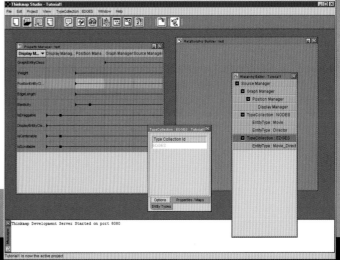

Multimedia communication is the next logical step of development after desktop publishing. Music clips and advertising spots are already teaching people the basics of multimedia. But writing in multimedia format needs to be practiced. The use of tools such as Powerpoint, the increasing spread of digital cameras and video-cutting software for amateurs are the first signs of this development.

your search terms:

Search Engines versus Serendipity

Search

internet 13039399

1 2 3 4 **5** 6 7 8 9

The Internet is growing by about 100,000 hosts per day. A large proportion of the knowledge which was stored in book form is now digitised and can be called up on the Internet. Almost all institutions, organisations and businesses are now represented on the Web.
In addition there are innumerable Internet-based companies, interest groups and private users. The organisational form of the Internet means that there is no master plan and no hierarchy.

Apart from the different quality of the connections used, the website of an 11-year-old Harry Potter fan in South Carolina who is looking for people with similar interests around the world is just as easy or difficult to access as the website of IBM.

This chapter deals with the subject of searching and finding on the Internet. What do search engines do? How do they work, and where are their limits? What alternative techniques are there to find one's way on the Internet and obtain worthwhile information?

Searching: The needle in the haystack

Results from three search engines which were given the same search task to perform.
Search query: Shaker. The search was for the religious community of that name in North America, which produces special furniture.

The results differ considerably. Whereas the first two search engines showed almost the same sites in an almost identical order, the results of the third search engine were completely different.

The results obtained with search engines are often frustrating. There are several reasons for this. First of all, it is not easy to formulate exactly what you are looking for.
To obtain useful results, you need to know what sort of questions or search queries can be rationally dealt with by a search engine.
The rule of thumb is: the more specific the question, the greater the likelihood of success.

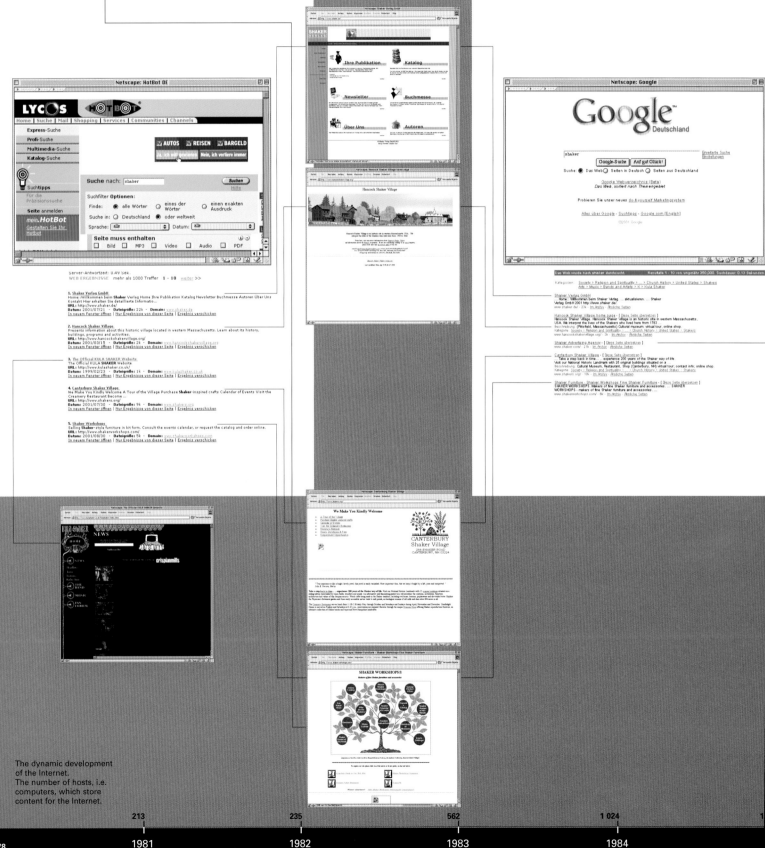

The dynamic development of the Internet.
The number of hosts, i.e. computers, which store content for the Internet.

213   235   562   1 024   1

1981   1982   1983   1984

For example, a search for information about a designer called Mario Bellini is likely to provide better results than a vague question which aims to learn "something about design". Search engines also differ in their methods of operation, and thus their search results. In addition to search engines which search through websites to determine where the same terms are used, such as Lycos, there are search engines which are edited and catalogued by people, such as Yahoo.

So-called metasearch engines consult several search engines at the same time to widen the radius of their search.

Work continues to refine the search methods in a quest to improve the quality of search results. The most powerful search engine at present is Google, which determines the relevance of its results by the number of links leading to the site found.

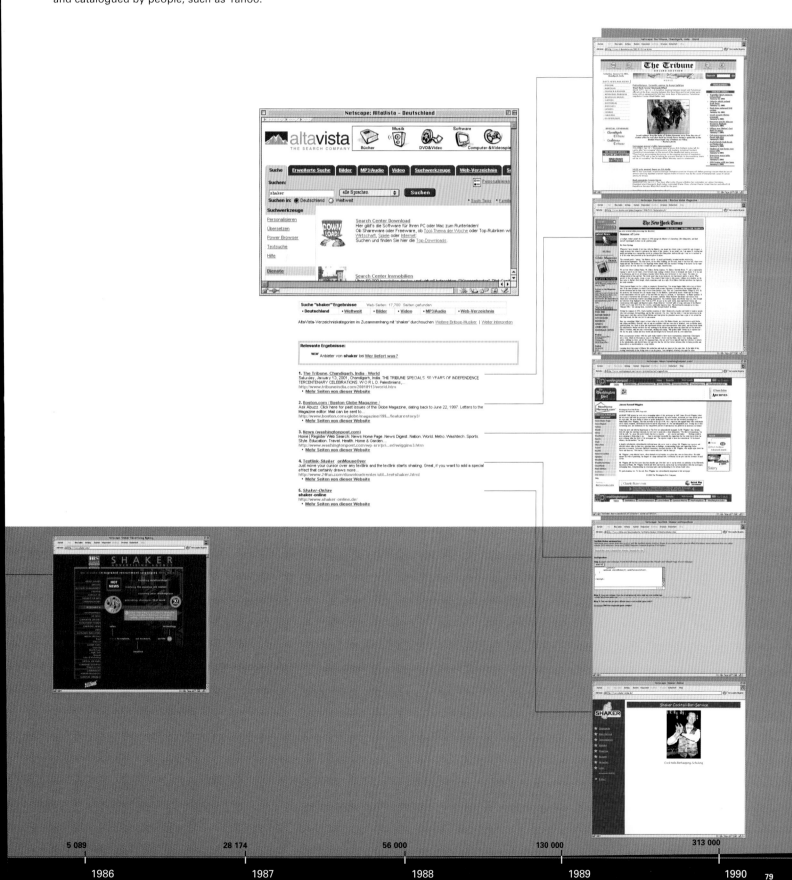

5 089   28 174   56 000   130 000   313 000

1986   1987   1988   1989   1990

Searching: calling things by name

The problem that users have with search engines is that they usually find too much. To filter out the really relevant information, the query must be systematically narrowed down and phrased in a way that is suitable for automatic processing.

Most search engines therefore offer additional search options which are based on mathematical principles of set theory. What makes communication with a search engine so difficult is the fact that the user must largely adapt to the search methods of a machine in order to be successful.

With so-called "Boolean" operations it is possible to link several terms logically so that intersections can be systematically searched for. These extended search functions are not always intuitive because the mathematical logic functions "and", "or" conflict with the use of the words in everyday speech.

Intersection: A and B (A^B)

Union: A or B (AvB)
colloquial : A and B

Difference: A and not B
(A \ B)

A xor B
colloquial : A or B

The dynamic development of the Internet. The number of hosts, i.e. computers, which store content for the Internet.

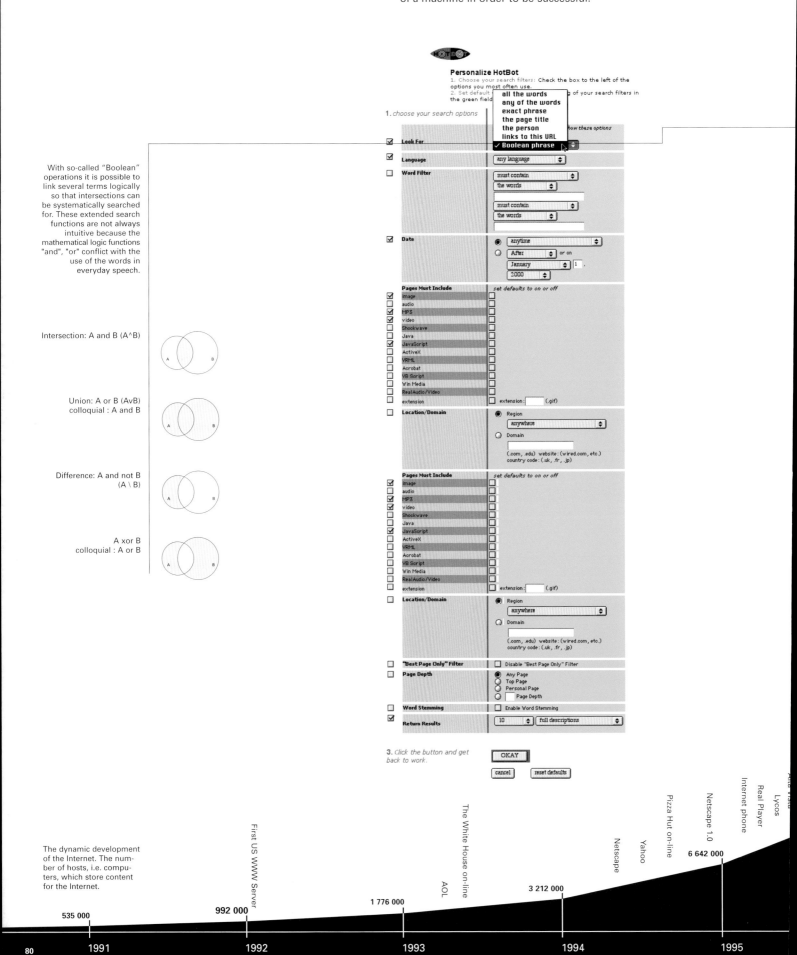

535 000   1991

992 000   First US WWW Server   1992

1 776 000   1993   AOL   The White House on-line

3 212 000   1994   Netscape   Yahoo   Pizza Hut on-line

6 642 000   Netscape 1.0   Internet phone   Real Player   Lycos   1995

The query forms which search engines offer
for their extended search can often not be
completed by the searcher, because he or
she is usually searching for something
because he or she does not yet know enough
about it to answer these questions precisely.

altavista
THE SEARCH COMPANY

Home > Advanced Search

Try these advanced searches: Images • Video • MP3/Audio

Boolean query:

`fruits and not apples`   any language

Use the terms AND, OR, AND NOT, NEAR.

Sort by:

(Enter terms to prioritize your results.)

Date: ○ by timeframe: Anytime

○ by date range: to   (dd/mm/yy)

Display: ☐ top few results per site

10 ◆ results per page

[Search]   Search Assistant | Basic Search

Examples

If you click on any of the following examples, you will immediately see that search made, live. Every search at AltaVista generates a
unique URL. That means that if there's a search you want to perform often, you can bookmark (add to Favorites) the results page,
and click on that link at any time see that same search again and get fresh results. We've used that feature to show you
these examples with live links, rather than static screen shots. Once you have clicked on an example, use the Back button on your
browser to return here.

When you enter a series of words, with no punctuation, AltaVista matches all pages on which any of those words appear. But the
pages that include all the terms you have entered appear near the top of the list, and those with fewer appear lower, and those
with only one go to the very bottom. In Boolean terms, it interprets your query as if the terms were separated by OR.

That means that instead of learning a bunch of commands with a "cheat sheet," you can simply enter a series of words, and have
confidence that the pages which are the best matches for you are likely to end up at the top of the list. In fact, in some cases, it's a
good strategy to enter many words related to what you want — even a dozen of more. Don't worry that the more words you enter,
the more matches AltaVista finds. It makes no difference whether there are 100,000 matches or a million. What matters is that the
most useful matches appear near the top of the list.

If you put a plus (+) sign in front of any word that means that that word must appear on a page for it to be a match. If there are
one or more terms that you want to exclude (in other words, you don't want to see pages on which these terms appear), place a
minus sign (-) in front of each of them.

Examples

harry potter quidditch

With no punctuation in the query, the software interprets harry potter as a phrase and quidditch as a separate word. Pages with
the phrase harry potter (those words together in that order) and quidditch will appear at the top of the match list. Then will appear
pages with all three of those words in any order.

"harry potter" +quidditch

The plus (+) sign means only include pages that contain the word quidditch. Quotation marks delineate a phrase. Pages with both
quidditch and the phrase "harry potter" would appear at the top of the list; then would come pages with quidditch but not "harry
potter." Pages with "harry potter" but not quidditch would not appear.

"harry potter" quidditch

This query matches all pages that have either the phrase harry potter or the word quidditch. Pages with both go to the top of the
list, so in most cases the top 200 results (which is what you see) will not differ from the above examples. But, technically speaking,
a page with just the phrase harry potter or just the word quidditch would be a match.

harry potter -quidditch
or
"harry potter" -quidditch

Both these queries yield pages on which the phrase harry potter appears and that do not contain the word quidditch.

Google: 1.000.000.000 documents indexed

Rich Media

Four out of five users never revisit a website

93 047 785

2.2 million websites = 300 000 000 Web pages

Napster

MS Explorer passes Navigator

Yahoo generates most search traffic

Turkmenistan sells Top Level Domain .tm

eBay goes public

56 218 000

Google.com

Netscape Sourcecode

Microsoft Explorer 4.0

Netscape Communicator

36 739 000

Car with Internet access

Real Video

Website of the CIA hacked

Netscape 3.0

Microsoft Explorer 3.0

Microsoft Explorer 2.0

19 540 000

000

**"The peculiarity of the new devices on the Internet is that you've got a double
acceleration or a double instability. First there's Moore's Law, the fact that the number
of processors on a chip, and thus computer power, keeps doubling every 18 months,
decade after decade.**

**Then there's Metcalfe's Law: the value of a net goes up as the square of the number of
people on that net. That is to say the Net itself or any net – even one made up of faxes
or cellular telephones –
increases dramatically in value the more people are on it.
You've got a double-runaway phenomenon.**

**Throw into that the tools that suddenly turn up, like the World Wide Web, Mosaic, and
later Netscape Navigator, which also can become dramatically empowering in short
order. The Net is a major social event. Culture's got to change."**

Stewart Brand

Site search

Many websites now offer search engines which only look for information from the same website.

This service is useful for extensive sites which are generated dynamically. Here, the individual pages are not created manually, but generated automatically from databases. For each individual query, the data are then loaded into a display mask which defines the graphical representation.

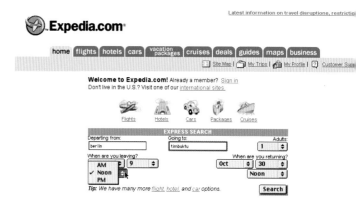

www.tonystone.com
The search engine of a picture archive. The selection of the pictures is achieved step-by-step by increasing specification. The number of pictures for selection is reduced until the final image is selected.

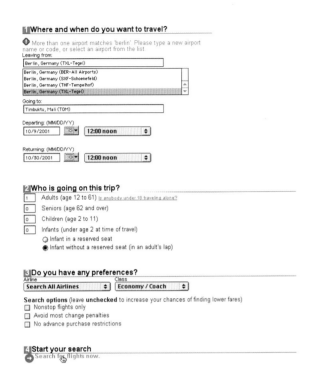

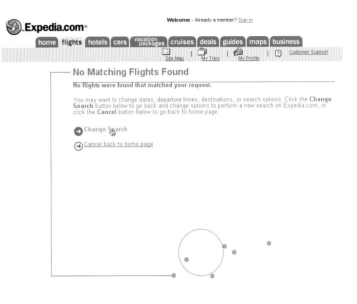

www.expedia.com
The booking search engine demands a precise query. The user's plans are more flexible than the search engine can cope with. This means that the user makes several attempts and, at best, lands lucky hits.

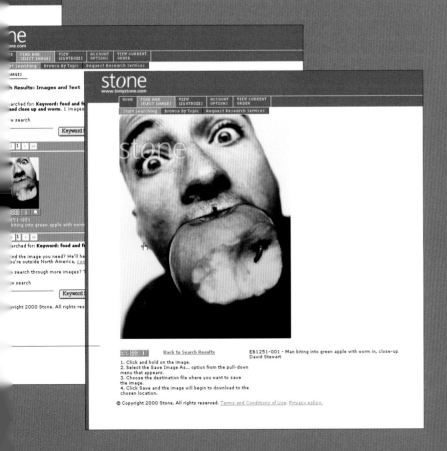

Many search engines play "battleships" with the user, i.e. the user must know what he or she is looking for and what it is called, and must have a pretty good idea that it is on that particular site, otherwise the user will not get any hits. The better search engines therefore offer ways to encircle the subject by guiding the user to go from the general to the specific in several search steps.

For sites which are updated daily, the search engine has proved to be an alternative to the site map because it also offers a powerful archiving function. The disadvantage of doing without a site map is that there is no clear overview of what the site contains. As navigation instruments, the search engine and site map supplement each other because they support the searching process in different ways.

Search engines of the next generation

The development in the search engines sector is moving increasingly towards more intelligent selection criteria, for example Google. There are also early attempts to adapt the design of the search to human search behaviour. For example, the graphical interface of the search engine Webbrain forms a mind map of the subject areas.

This graphical representation depicts the search path and the context. This enables complete misinterpretations of the term to be avoided. At each point in the search it is possible to open out the search again if it becomes apparent that the search has taken the wrong path.

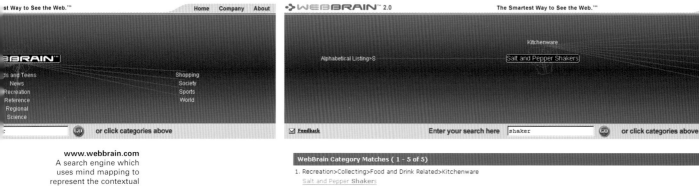

www.webbrain.com
A search engine which uses mind mapping to represent the contextual meaning of the term searched for.

WebBrain Category Matches (1 - 5 of 5)

1. Recreation>Collecting>Food and Drink Related>Kitchenware
   Salt and Pepper Shakers
2. Society>Religion and Spirituality>Christianity>Church History>United States
   Shakers
3. Arts>Music>Bands and Artists>Alphabetical Listing>K
   Kula Shaker
4. Regional>North America>United States>Ohio>Localities>Alphabetical Listing>S
   Shaker Heights
5. Regional>North America>United States>Ohio>Localities>Alphabetical Listing>C>Cleveland>Neighborhoods
   Buckeye-Shaker Square

WebBrain Site Matches (1 - 15 of 333)

1. 2000 Shaker Workshops Photography Competitions
   Competition in 2 categories: interior shots, exterior shots Photographs must highlight **Shaker** architecture, **Shaker** furniture and accessories in real life. Pictures may be from both **Shaker** sites or other sites. Postal mail entries, black and white, color, slides or prints accepted. Very high standards of photography shown, see site for previous winners. First prize in each category receives gift certificate and image will be published.
   http://www.**shaker**workshops.com/photog.htm Arts>Photography>Contests

www.sinnzeug.de
An experimental catalogue which dynamically represents associative links between the terms searched for in the form of hyperlinks.

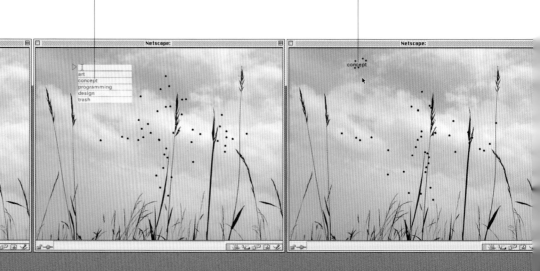

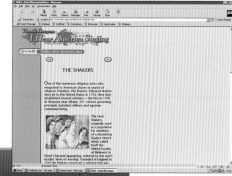

>WEBBRAIN™ 2.0   The Smartest Way to See the Web.™

Alphabetical Listing>S
W>Watervliet

United States

Shakers

Music

☑ Feedback   Enter your search here [   ] GO   or click categories above

Print Results

Society>Religion and Spirituality>Christianity>Church History>United States>Shakers (1 - 20 of 25)

1. Wonders Movement - A comparison of doctrine from the Shaker precedent, today's extremist counterpart, and a New Testament example.
   http://www.discernment.org/some.htm

2. Canterbury Shaker Village - Cultural Museum, Restaurant, Shop (Canterbury, NH) virtual tour; contact info; online shop.
   http://www.shakers.org/index.html

3. Connecticut Cane and Reed Company: Shaker books - Book sales; links.
   http://www.caneandreed.com/shakerbooks.html

4. Hancock Shaker Village - (Pittsfield, Massachusetts) Cultural museum: virtual tour, online shop.
   http://www.hancockshakervillage.org/

5. IHAS - The Shakers - A brief history of the Shaker movement, including their cultural and musical contributions.
   http://www.pbs.org/wnet/ihas/icon/shakers.html

6. Keegan's Place - The Shakers - Includes a bibliography and excerpts from the diary of a member of the sect.
   http://users.neca.com/keegans/shakers.html

7. Mount Lebanon Shaker Village - (New Lebanon, NY) includes a brief overview and tourist information.
   http://hometown.aol.com/annaly75/homepage.html

In the experimental search engines sector, attempts are being made to use and represent hypertext structures. In most of these attempts, the third dimension is used for the representation. This creates new design challenges, because representing the third dimension on a two-dimensional screen creates a new form of visual confusion.

Other approaches in this sector include learning systems such as agent systems. The aim here is to improve the quality of search results by creating and evaluating the user profile. And research queries can be sent off into the Internet in the form of agents, small programs which operate independently.

The term **"surfing the Internet"** graphically describes the associative links on the Web. As there is no general, up-to-date and reliable overview, and often not even stable and fast connections on the Internet, **chance** is a major factor.

The starting point is often just to have another look at the introductory page to see what has changed since the last visit. But links, advertisements and long loading times can quickly lead users to forget the original route. The element of surprise and the possibility of finding valuable information without even looking for it are significant features. Search engines are a logical starting point, but it is sometimes possible to find things on a hunch by deducing a www address from a term or a name.

The phrase "surfing the Internet" was coined by Jean Armour in 1992.

ser·en·dip·i·ty (srn-dp-t)
n. pl. ser·en·dip·i·ties

1. The faculty of making fortunate discoveries by accident.
2. The fact or occurrence of such discoveries.
3. An instance of making such a discovery.

[From the characters in the Persian fairy tale The Three Princes of Serendip, who made such discoveries, from Persian Sarandp, Sri Lanka, from Arabic sarandb.]

seren·dipi·tous adj.
seren·dipi·tous·ly adv.

Word History: We are indebted to the English author Horace Walpole for the word serendipity, which he coined in one of the 3,000 or more letters on which his literary reputation primarily rests. In a letter of January 28, 1754, Walpole says that "this discovery, indeed, is almost of that kind which I call Serendipity, a very expressive word." Walpole formed the word from an old name for Sri Lanka, Serendip. He explained that this name was part of the title of "a silly fairy tale, called The Three Princes of Serendip: as their highnesses travelled, they were always making discoveries, by accidents and sagacity, of things which they were not in quest of…"

A number of rules for the planning and design of a website can be derived from surfing techniques. The initial loading time must not strain the patience of the visitor, and it must be possible to see how much time remains. Any introductory pages are a hindrance on a second visit, and it should be possible to skip them.

Personalisation is a further way to avoid frustrating the visitor. Whatever the content, the website should have a certain entertainment value. To do justice to the medium, it should have a certain topical nature to encourage repeated visits.

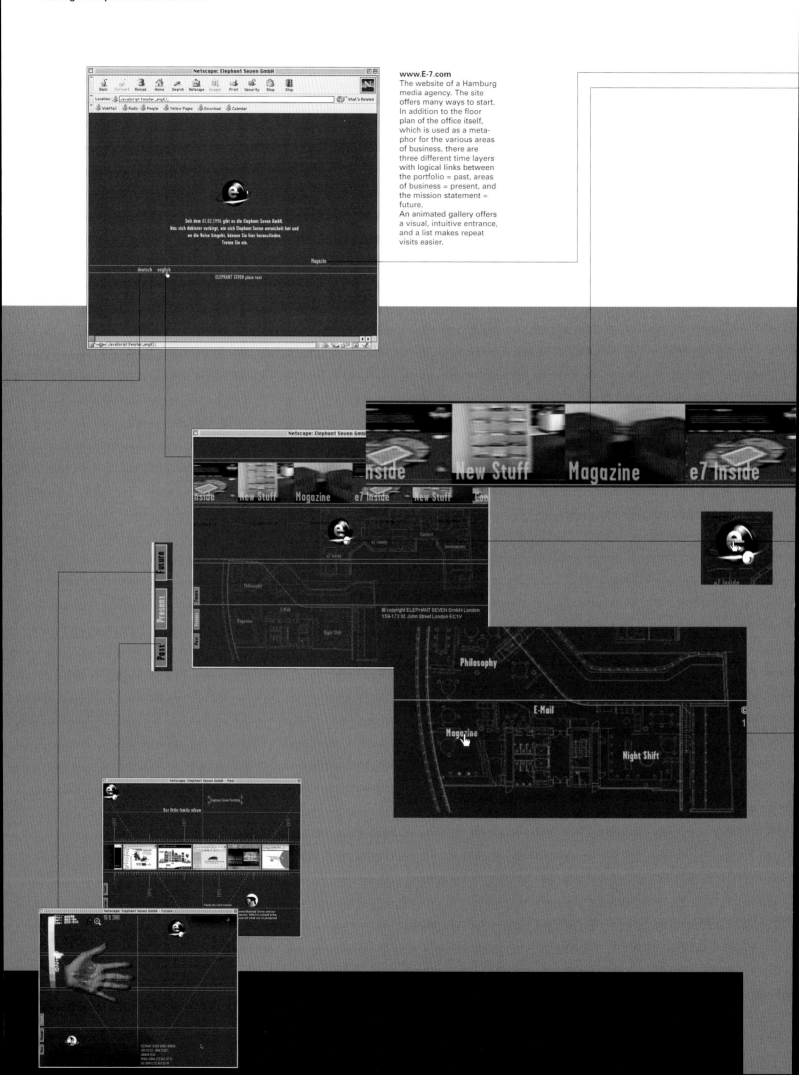

www.E-7.com
The website of a Hamburg
media agency. The site
offers many ways to start.
In addition to the floor
plan of the office itself,
which is used as a meta-
phor for the various areas
of business, there are
three different time layers
with logical links between
the portfolio = past, areas
of business = present, and
the mission statement =
future.
An animated gallery offers
a visual, intuitive entrance,
and a list makes repeat
visits easier.

Redundancy in the information structure is desirable. The possibility of reaching specific content in different ways exists in this medium and should be used. Systematic searching needs a different presentation of information than casual browsing and "strolling" through the information.
If the user wants to get to know an unknown site, resources such as site maps, guided tours and menu structures are helpful, but if the user is searching for specific information on the site, a search engine may be the best tool.

If a metaphor is used to present the available information in a narrative framework, a list which shows the available information again is a helpful form of redundancy.

Site maps support the visitor's memory by imposing a structure on the content displayed. This structure is easier to "archive" than a collection of words.

Repeat visits

see also pages 66|67

Lesezeichen

Lesezeichen hinzufügen	⌘D
Lesezeichen bearbeiten	⌘B

Wegweiser ▶

imke ▶
Persönliche Symbolleiste-Ordner
Live Home Page
Suchen
Macintosh Produktkatalog

Apple ▶
Unterstützung und Informationen ▶
Veröffentlichungen über Macintosh ▶
Hardware- und Software-Händler ▶
Software-Entwickler ▶
Hardware-Entwickler ▶
Multimedia ▶

Eigene Bookmarks
navibook ▶
Untitled Document
7_5mockup10
7_5mockup10
7_5mockup10
7_5.html
404 Not Found
index
Quark Incorporated
Quark: Download Results
Quark: Download Results
gravis.de - Coming home!
HotBot DE
Yahoo!
Sign in - Yahoo! Mail
lap6
Google
Dictionary Search Englisch-Deutsch
Langenscheidts Fremdwörterbuch online
Google
NewsMaps.com Shows Visual Landscapes of News
Free SpeedScript: the speedway to new DHTML and Ja...
Internet Einfuehrung
Google-Suche: webhistory
Google-Suche: webseiten wachstum
Suchmaschinen - Teoma
deutsche Suchmaschinen
Suchmaschinen Expertenportal wer-weiss-was, www.we...
Google-Suche: informationsflut
Kampf gegen die Informationsflut
menu.w3history.phtml
sources.de.phtml
Internet Domain Survey
Amazon.de
Nua Internet Surveys : Graphs & Charts - 1998
Übersicht - Zahlen & Fakten
Internet Software Consortium - Number of Internet ...
pReview - digital design

List of bookmarks as
displayed in the browser
Netscape Navigator 4.7.

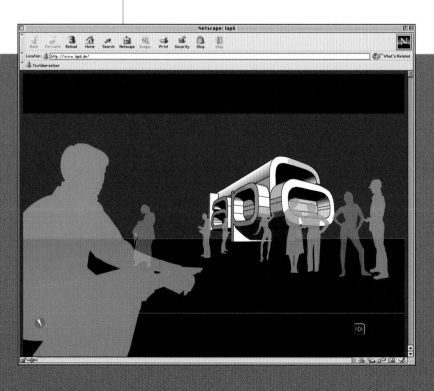

One of the most difficult tasks in the Internet is to go back to something you have previously discovered. This is partly because it is a dynamic medium, a permanent building site – but also because the aids to memory in today's browsers are not very well developed. The option of retracing one's steps within a browser session only works within a single browser window.

The option of setting bookmarks is a guessing game because of the inconsistent designation of the archived links. And bookmarks to dynamic pages do not work at all. No visual identification of any kind is used when archiving the links. It would be desirable, for example, to archive the surfing path and bookmarks in the form of **thumbnails** such as those we find in application programs.

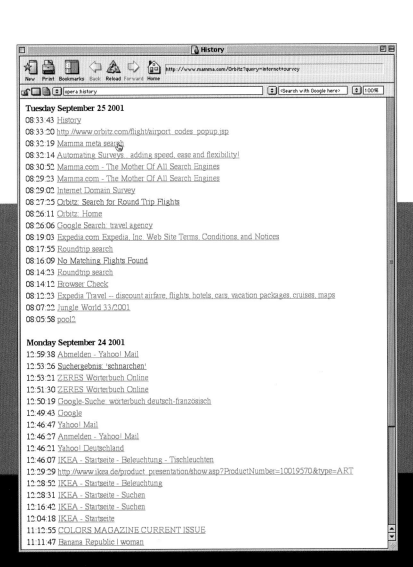

In the browser Opera 5.0, the sites that have been visited are archived as a history in a chronological list irrespective of which browser window they were displayed in.

The Parallel Universe

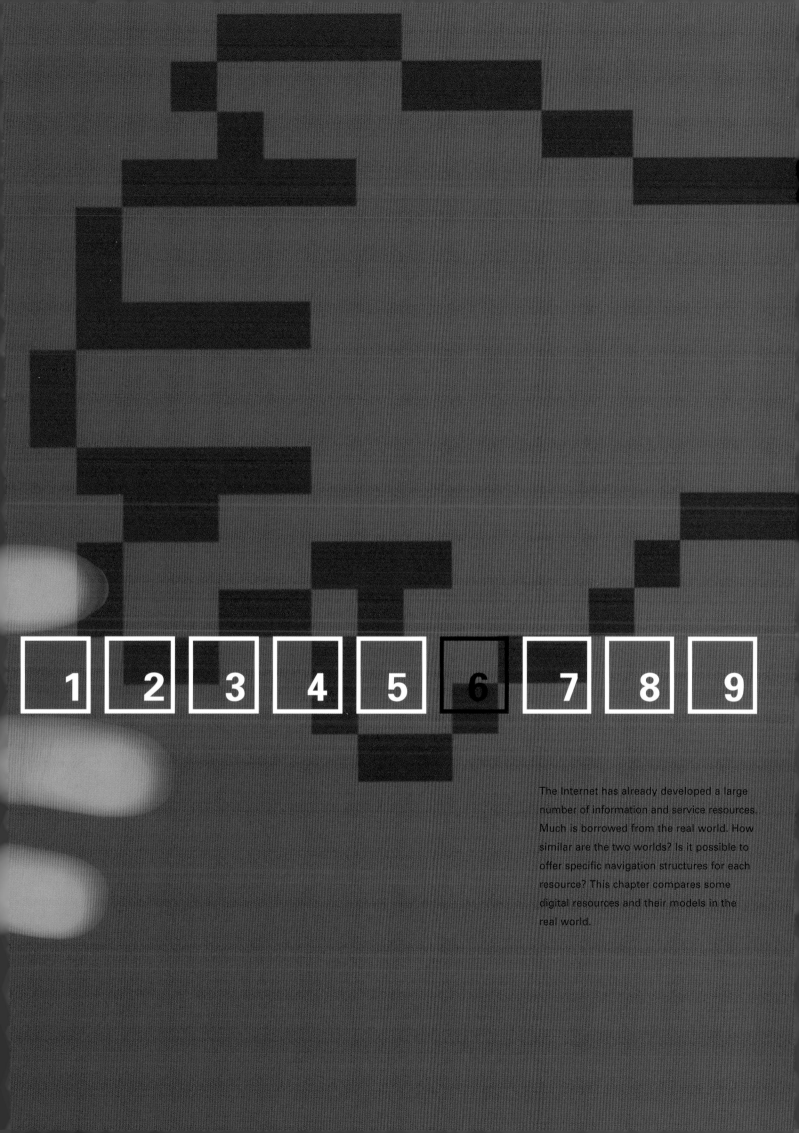

1 2 3 4 5 **6** 7 8 9

The Internet has already developed a large number of information and service resources. Much is borrowed from the real world. How similar are the two worlds? Is it possible to offer specific navigation structures for each resource? This chapter compares some digital resources and their models in the real world.

Letter and e-mail

This comparison in particular shows that the digital counterpart is an enrichment.

In spite of all the critics, this example clearly demonstrates that technical progress rarely leads to an "either/or" decision, and usually involves a "both/and" option instead.

The new medium enables the traditional medium to regain its specific qualities.

The possibility to deal with a large proportion of necessary correspondence by e-mail restores "old-fashioned" letter writing as a deliberate activity which ranges from the choice of paper to the selection of the stamp. The handwritten original is appreciated in a new way.

"E-mail is like coming home at night after a long day and finding 70 people in your kitchen."
John O'Donohue

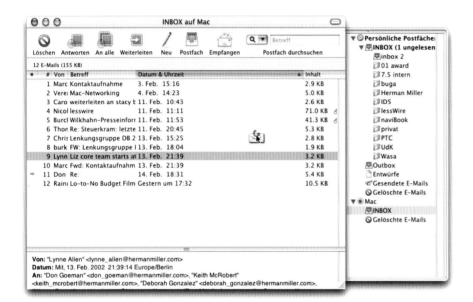

Apple OSX Mail
An e-mail program which is closely based on the icons of letter writing.

Basic happy
Japanese style.

Löschen Antworten An alle Weiterleiten Neu Postfach Empfangen

E-mail as a communication tool, with its icons of the letter box and envelope, closely follow the physical model. The speed of the medium and the ability to make digital copies and archives make e-mail so successful. Typographical refinery is superfluous because the sender usually does not know on what system and with what software the recipient will read the e-mail.

This leads to considerable differences in the display of what is written.

Because of its speed, e-mail resembles an oral dialogue rather than the exchange of written documents. This is reflected in the style in which e-mail texts are written: they are in more everyday language and are often supplemented by **emoticons**.

bcc: blind carbon copy
A copy to another recipient which is unseen by the primary recipient: "For your information...".

cc: carbon copy
A term that means the same in e-mails as it does on traditional paper-based office communication: "Copy to...".

www.jetzt.de
E-cards simulate the ability to send individually designed mail.

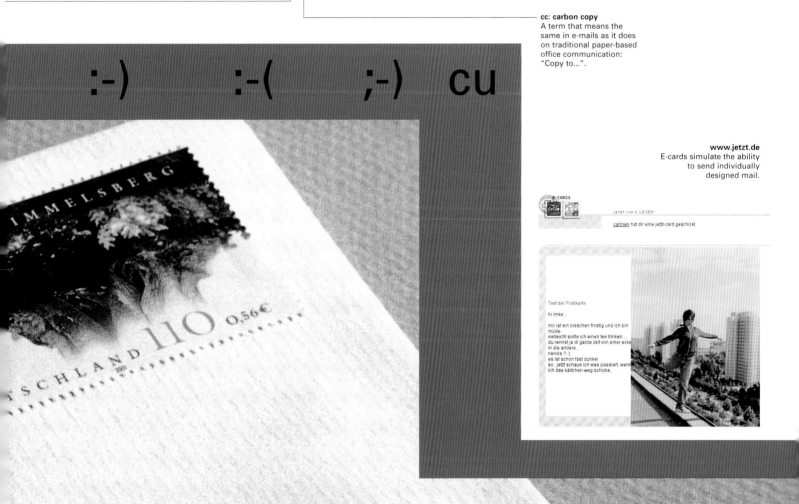

Here, too, the co-existence of the two forms leads to a sharpening of the profile. The classical bookshop must make use of the fact that the customer is physically present. A strategy which is observed more and more frequently. Bookshops are being fitted out as literary oases in which customers can spend hours drinking coffee and browsing through books.

The success of the Internet bookshop Amazon is due to the way it interprets the characteristics of a good bookshop for the Internet. By contrast with clothing, sending books by mail order is not a great risk. But the virtual nature of the transactions still has disadvantages which need to be compensated for.

Amazon.com

Amazon.com opened its virtual doors in 1995 with the vision of using the Internet to make buying books into a simple, fast and pleasant shopping experience. Amazon is now represented in 220 countries, and in addition to books, its range of products now includes CDs, DVDs, computers and electronic goods.

The presentation of the individual book is closely based on the real model – in addition to the title it is also possible to see the cover texts, the list of contents and a selection of the inside pages.

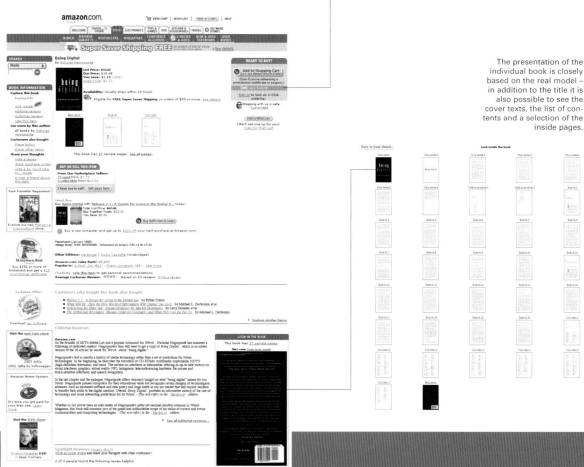

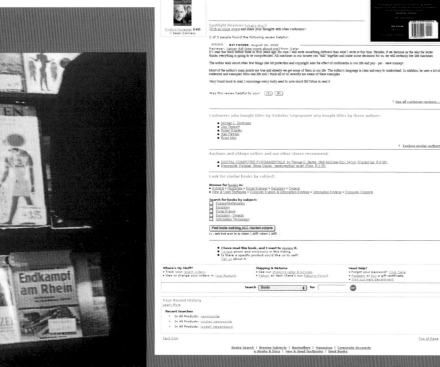

The experience of browsing and finding things by chance is compensated by the creation and updating of a user profile. When a registered customer visits Amazon, the first page that is loaded, the "shop window", is decorated with titles that may be of interest to the visitor.

Like at the bookshop round the corner, the payment can be initiated by just saying that you want to buy a book, and the "first click" system uses the banking details that have already been registered. The delivery and gift service follow conveniently after the payment process, and all known addresses are offered for selection.

E-mail communication informs the customer of the status of the dispatch procedure at all times and compensates for the delay of not walking out of the shop with the book physically in your hand.

Again, all of the advantages of the medium are harnessed in the search for subjects, titles or authors. They include the possibility to read or write readers' reviews.

The book and the electronic book

The electronic book is becoming more established. Product descriptions of electronic devices and software manuals are increasingly being supplied on CD-ROM in PDF format (portable document format). It is left to the user to print it out on paper.

These digital books are actually printed in many cases. This is because reading on screen is still a strenuous activity.

The comparatively low resolution, the frequency and contrast of CRT computer monitors, LCD or TFT flat screens do not permit fatigue-free reading.

Books have a physical, tactile quality, they need no electricity, are comparatively robust and offer high quality reproductions.

This is the reason why the present subject is so suitable for the classical medium of the book: the book facilitates synchronous optical presentations to show different items of information alongside each other for comparison.

"The book is a garden that you can carry in your pocket."
Arabic proverb

Reading novels in bed or in the bath will also continue to be a paper-based activity due to the lack of any competitive alternative.

Navigating through a document in PDF format is closely based on the technique of browsing through the pages of a book. The pages can be turned with the back and forward buttons.

To provide an overview of the quantity of the text and the "thickness" of the book, the **variable zoom** can be used as a navigation technique. The pages are reduced in size until they can all be displayed on the monitor. Due to **visual pattern recognition**, it is possible to find text passages even at the smallest size.

see also pages 40|41

see also pages 66|67

committed to developing a unique site
and what influence – if any – there is
from competitors.

Finally – and perhaps most impor-
tantly – profit implications of our in-
terviews seem to point toward the fact
that revenue models will be "locally"
driven. "Local" in this case means that
each newspaper seems to be finding its
own way toward profitability or failure. Indeed, even the word "model"
seems to be mis-used, since it implies
that a profit mechanism can successfully be used elsewhere. Although we
saw different newspapers use different
schemes, there seemed to be an experimental mentality in most cases, since
few were truly profitable.

The process of underlining
and commenting on
interesting passages is
closely based on the
physical model.

Bookmarks can be placed,
and extensive comments
can be added.

PDF format is in the process
of becoming a full substitute
for printed paper.
Techniques such as the
digital signature are even
making PDF files eligible
as official documents.

Browsing.

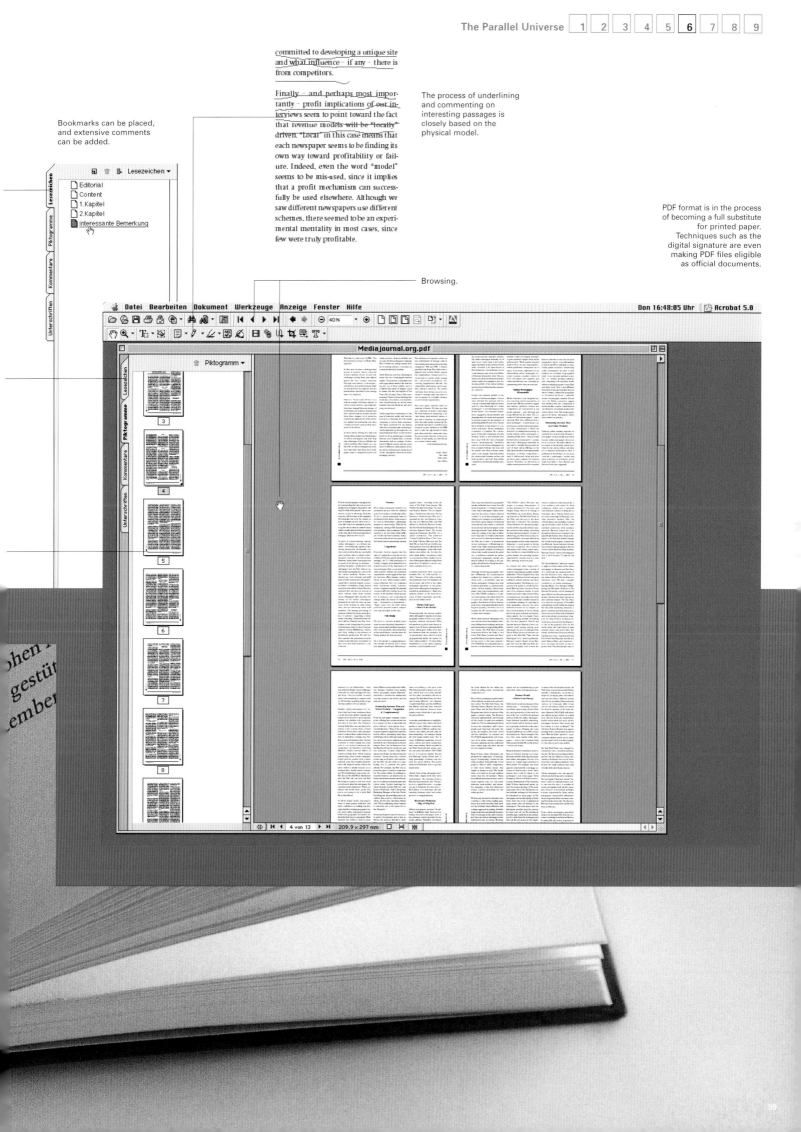

The daily newspaper and its website

The daily newspaper is finding it difficult to compete with its digital counterpart. It has already been overtaken by television in providing up-to-date news, and the results in relation to the Internet are similar. Immediate updates and live transmissions make on-line newspapers immensely up to date. Small adverts, which were a major sales argument for the print edition, are also being increasingly offered on the Internet.

The advantage of the print version is the established, classical distribution network – the information is transmitted digitally, then decentrally converted into physical form and distributed – until it can be bought on every street corner.

The layout of a daily newspaper offers a highly sophisticated, visual structure of the information presented. The strong contrast in type sizes offers different modes of reading such as fast scanning or detailed reading.

Today's columns

Guardian columnists

Observer columnists

It's time for a new bottom line: a spiritual dimension
Jonathan Freedland: Giving up smoking? Wimp. Vowing to shed the pounds? Loser. More regular trips to the gym? Skipping dessert? You're a big girl's blouse. Changing the world? That's different. That's a serious new year's resolution.

The daily newspaper on the Internet takes its structure from its classical counterpart. Unfortunately, however, the visual differentiation of the information by using vastly different type sizes is not preserved in the design of the Internet versions.

The special properties of the medium, for example its topicality, lead to formal and structural changes. Where it was formerly a matter of prestige to write the leading article, the articles on the website are structured and presented in chronological order.

Archiving is an extra advantage of the medium: all earlier articles on the same subject can be called up directly.

"Above the fold"
Like a physical newspaper, the most important information is presented at the top and visible without scrolling.

interactive guide
Background information is presented in multimedia form for better understanding.

www.guardian.co.uk
After a provisional version which was launched in 1994, the Guardian has been on-line since 1999 as the "Guardian unlimited network of websites".

"The trouble with newspapers is that they are a mile wide and an inch deep. Websites that work best are an inch wide and a mile deep."

Paul Zwillenberg

The television station and its website

The website of a television station is significantly different in structure from its broadcast counterpart, and thus supplements it. Whereas the sequential medium of television broadcasts the information sequentially in various programme patterns, the website provides this information concurrently. The programme formats only provide the titles for the categories of the website.

www.cnn.com
The news portal of the television station of the same name, with regional editions and in several languages. By contrast with television, it is possible to select your regional version on the Internet.

As these two principles are at present still transmitted on two different platforms, there is not yet any synergy between the "push" medium of television and the "pull" medium of the computer. If a television programme includes a reference to further information on the Internet, the viewer must note down the address and start the computer and browser to access this information.

The structure and navigation of newspaper and television station sites are very similar. The secondary use of film contributions in the form of digital film sequences on television station sites represents a competitive advantage.

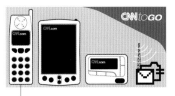

see also pages 146|147

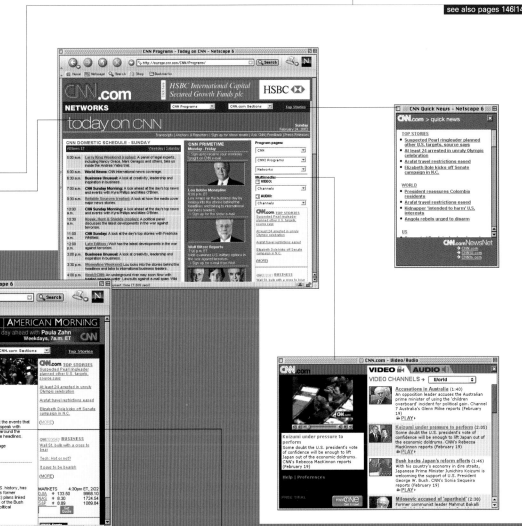

"Television: a medium. So called because it is neither rare nor well done."
Ernie Kovacs

Lou Dobbs is the anchor and managing editor of CNN's Lou Dobbs Moneyline. A founding member of the network in 1980 as well as CNN's financial news division, Dobbs spent 19 years with CNN before leaving in 1999 to launch SPACE.com, the first multimedia company dedicated to space and space-related content. He returned to CNN in 2001 to his current position. Dobbs also anchors a financial news radio report, which is syndicated by United Stations Radio Networks, Inc. to 785 stations nationwide.

Dobbs became anchor of Moneyline the year he joined CNN, and was instrumental in making Moneyline the most prestigious business news program in history. During his tenure at the network, he helped develop CNN financial news to the award-winning leader in television business journalism, and oversaw the launch of CNNfn in December 1995. He managed the network as president of CNNfn and executive vice president of CNN until June 1999.

Dobbs has won nearly every major award for television journalism. He received the George Foster Peabody Award for his coverage of the 1987 stock market crash. In 1990, he was given the Luminary Award by the Business Journalism Review for his "visionary work which changed the landscape of business journalism in the 1980s." His other honors include CableACE, Front Page, Janus and Emmy awards. In 1999, he won the Horatio Alger Association Award for Distinguished Americans and, in 2000, the National Space Club Media Award.

Dobbs graduated from Harvard University with a degree in economics. He serves on the boards of the Society of Professional Journalists Foundation, the Horatio Alger Association, the National Space Foundation and SPACE.com, in which he owns a minority stake, as he does in Integrity Bank. He is also a member of the Planetary Society, the Overseas Press Club, the American Economic Association and the National Academy of Television Arts & Sciences.

Travel agents and Internet travel services

Booking travel on the Internet would be a sensible application – the user can decide at home in peace how he or she wants to spend his or her holiday – but in actual fact, this area is a prime example of how the two worlds can rival each other. The Internet threatens traditional sales channels with guaranteed profit margins and territorial protection. Therefore many travel packages – with the exception of last minute deals – are far more expensive than when they are booked traditionally via the travel agent.

see also pages 82|83

Moreover, many Internet presentations frustrate users with slow loading times, clumsy entry masks and unimaginative **search categories**, for example by requiring the codes of international airports instead of the names of the towns and cities.

www.opodo.com
The Internet travel service Opodo ("Opportunity to do") operated by nine European airlines offers flight bookings, car hire, hotel reservations and travel insurance. In addition there is a travel guide which provides basic information about the country in question. Reviews by other users could add life to the website, but they are hardly used.

Little use is made of the visualisation of information. The user must have a globe and the basic geographical data available, e.g. the seasons and average temperatures, in order to plan his journey.

www.super-last-minute.de
Travel service of L`Tur which uses the medium to appeal particularly to last minute travellers. The L`Tur weather machine offers an original search criterion: by entering the temperature, the user can search for all destinations where it is warmer than 23 degrees.

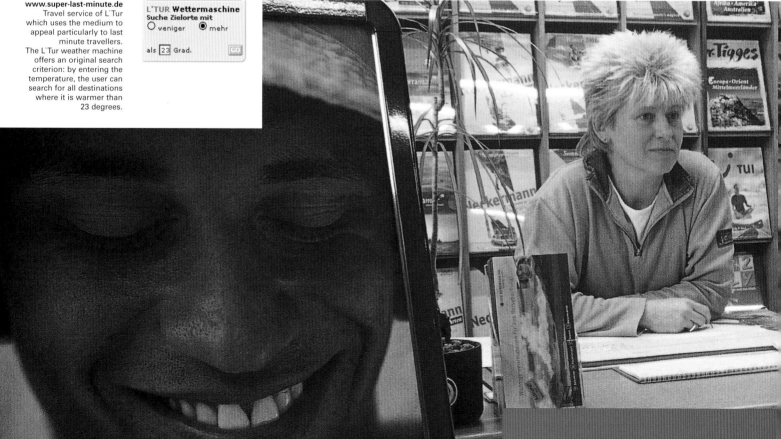

The user has to engage in unnecessary repetitive operations: for example, if he subsequently reserves a car, he must enter all the travel data again.

The packages on offer are displayed in long scrollable lists which make direct comparisons difficult. The only item which can be seen quickly is the airline code.

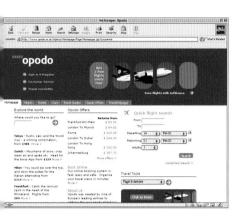

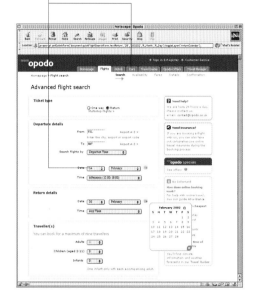

The foundation of the Internet auction service eBay in 1995 under the motto "Auctions for all" has made auctions a popular sport. This newly created service uses the medium of the Internet effectively by creating a platform on which goods can be traded in an elaborate manner.

The goods can be searched worldwide by categories. To ascertain the value of the goods, the auction principle is used.

Traditionally, auctions are an elaborate process which is restricted in time and limited to certain groups of goods. The transfer to the digital medium means that anyone can buy or sell goods of all kinds by auction. All auctions proceed concurrently on a time schedule defined by the vendor. Like a flea market, this wide range of goods in all price brackets makes users browse.

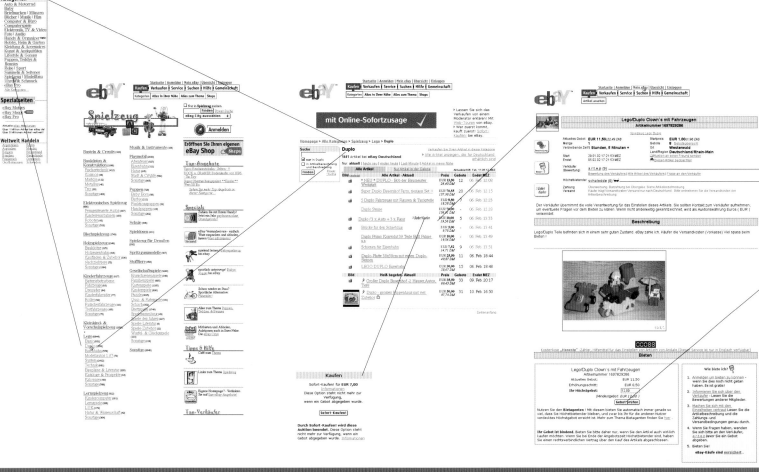

"Auctioneer: The man who proclaims with a hammer that he has picked a pocket with his tongue."
Ambrose Bierce

The navigation at eBay is designed to help the potential user lose his or her fear of digital trading. To this end, eBay has developed various services such as the ID card which provides information on the business habits of a potential trading partner.

New eBay member
10 to 99
100 to 499
500 to 999
1,000 to 4,999
5,000 to 9,999
10,000 to 24,999
25,000 to 49,999
50,000 to 99,999
100,000 and more
Certified member

Vendors are evaluated by a points system. New members are especially highlighted, and professionals can have themselves certified. All of these measures help to replace real rituals, to create trust in the virtual environment and to provide guidance.

The help functions are not placed in a separate area, instead they are integrated into every page in the form of questions.

Mental Models, Metaphors and Cyberworlds

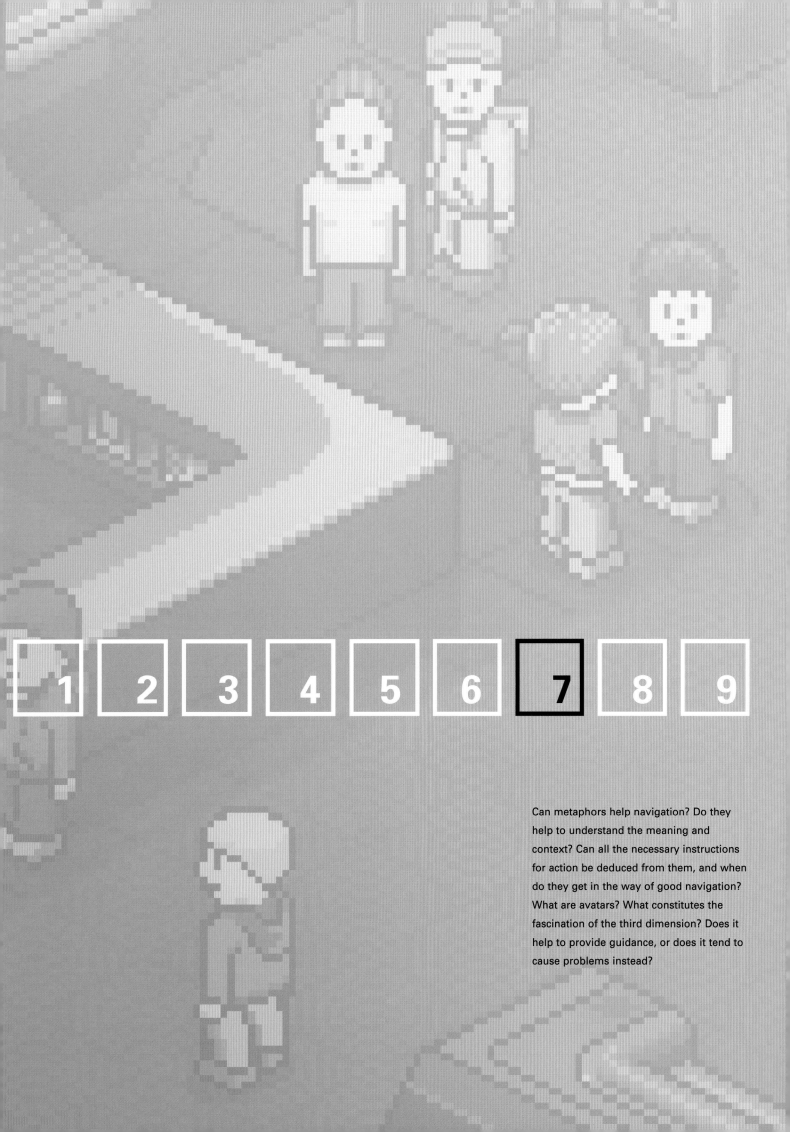

Can metaphors help navigation? Do they help to understand the meaning and context? Can all the necessary instructions for action be deduced from them, and when do they get in the way of good navigation? What are avatars? What constitutes the fascination of the third dimension? Does it help to provide guidance, or does it tend to cause problems instead?

see also pages 64|65

Mental models play a major role in digital systems. The new can only be learned by making connections to what is already known. At the operating system level, **icons** reflect all the components of the interface; in applications they take the form of **tools** which visualise the program routines. Here, too, both aspects of icons are used – non-verbal communication and integrated instructions for action. The icon is not always immediately and unambiguously understandable. As an introduction, contextual aids which help the user interpret them in the learning phase are useful.

;-)

The mood of a message is very hard to convey via text only.
So called "emoticons" are a shorthand way of explaining the meaning without the intonation of one´s voice.

With the improvement of the display on screens, the development of icons has to some extent moved in opposite directions. In desktop display, a more concrete definition of abstract concepts can be observed – this is illustrated here by the development of the "Delete" function in the operating system MacOS.

1984

1991

1996

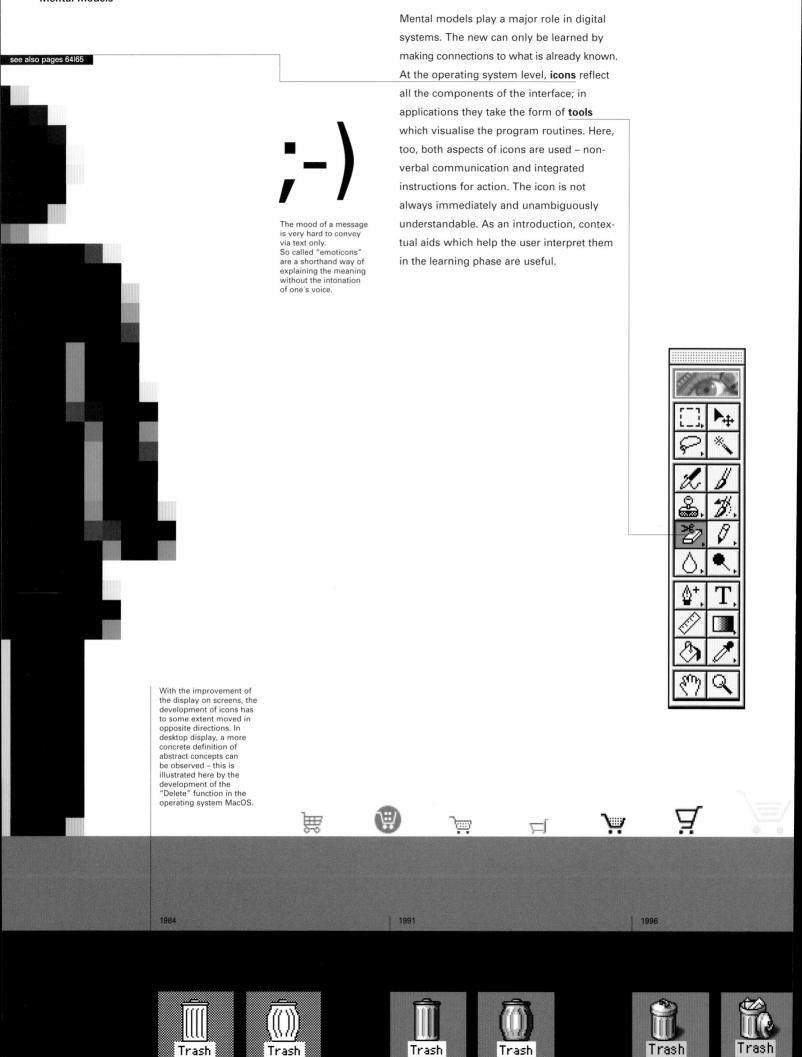

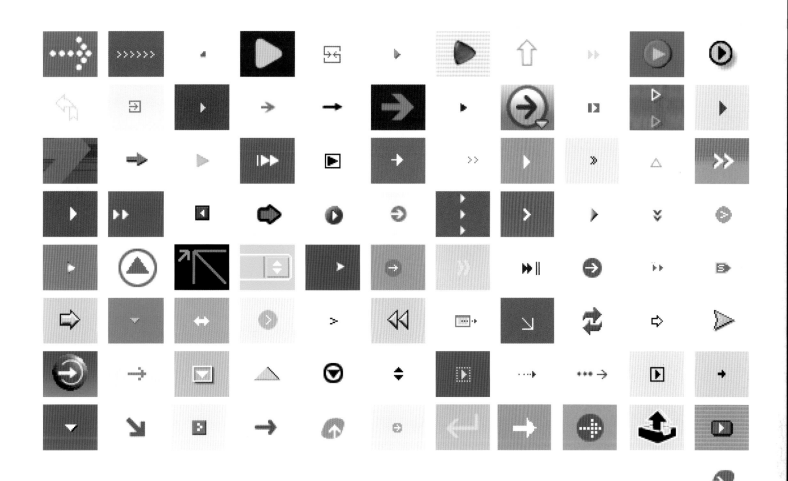

The icon of a shopping trolley conveys a comprehensive action model which is familiar from real life. The user can place the goods they are interested in and wish to buy in the shopping trolley, and when they want to finish any purchases, they then initiate the payment process. But as in real life, the user can also take goods out of the trolley or simply leave the trolley without buying the goods.

www.bloomingdales.com
The familiar big brown bag is used as an icon for collecting and buying goods instead of the shopping trolley. This does not correspond exactly to the significance of the shopping trolley, but it is understood.

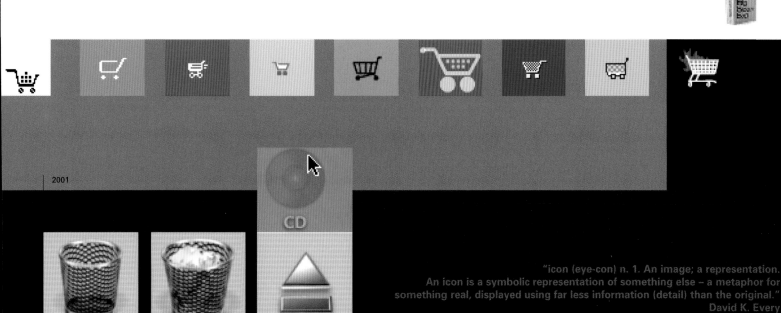

2001

CD

"icon (eye-con) n. 1. An image; a representation. An icon is a symbolic representation of something else – a metaphor for something real, displayed using far less information (detail) than the original."
David K. Every

Symbolic actions

Icons with the instructions for action which they contain can be grouped into combined actions. To define a combined action, a metaphor is often used which places the individual program routines into a meaningful context that can be understood by the user. The desktop metaphor in modern operating systems is such a metaphor.

It uses the elements of an office workplace to visualise data structures as documents and directory structures as folders. Techniques such as "drag and drop" corresponding to the **intuitive, direct manipulation** of data, dragging a document on to the "trash" icon means "deleting the data".

The metaphor can even take into account the "real world" possibility of making a mistake. Even on the computer, a document that has been placed in the "waste paper basket" can be taken out again. The file is only actually deleted when the "trash" is emptied. These actions are valuable mnemonic tricks which follow the same learning strategies as in the real world.

see also pages 30|31

"Doing with images makes symbols." Alan Kay

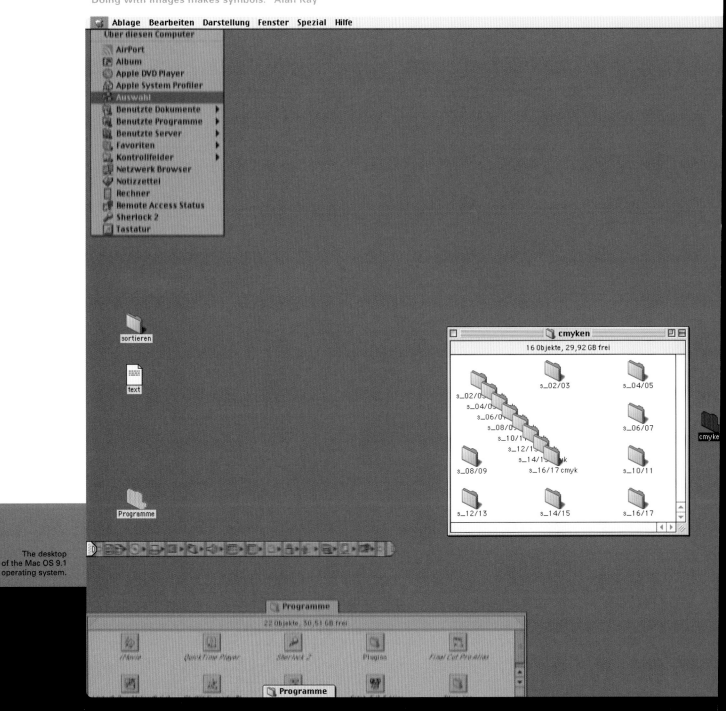

The desktop of the Mac OS 9.1 operating system.

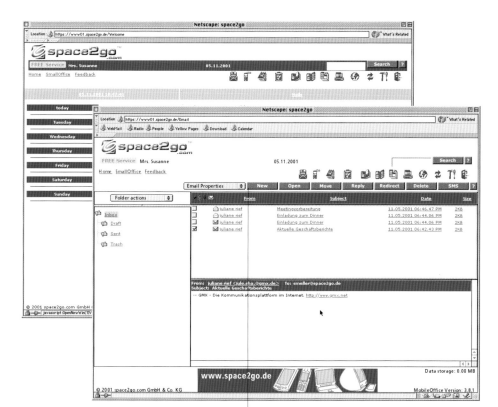

www.space2go.com
On-line working
environment with
synchronisation of
different end devices.

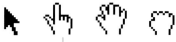

On the Internet, the interaction culture is normally restricted to **"point and click"**. This is mainly for technical reasons; fully interactive sites are only possible if sophisticated scripts are integrated. However, the more clearly the websites offer services and have the character of tools, the more often they will be compared with the interaction culture of local applications.

To avoid frustration, the instructions for action must be simple, understandable and unambiguous. In the design, it must be ensured that interactive elements are clearly identified as such and can be distinguished from elements that are purely for information. The three-dimensional display of interactive elements, for example in the form of buttons, has become an established feature.
In addition or as an alternative, context-sensitive **cursor change** can indicate possible interactions and provide instructions for action.

"Tell me and I forget.
Teach me and I remember.
Involve me and I learn."
Benjamin Franklin

The opportunities and limitations of metaphors

Metaphors are framework actions which place all the individual components into a logical context. It is often difficult to extend metaphors if new functions need to be integrated: either the new functions are omitted because it is not possible to integrate them rationally, or the new functions are integrated but there are logical inconsistencies in the system which can no longer be explained by the metaphor.

MagicLink
Personal Digital Assistant
by Sony (1993).

MagicCap
Software for MagicLink.

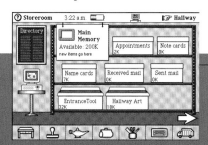

Data storage

Address management

The desktop

On-line banking

The more naturalistic the metaphor is, the more difficult it becomes to explain functions that are only possible in a virtual context. The concept of the alias, i.e. one or more access points to a computer file, is difficult to convey in the digital world because it has no counterpart in the real world.

Private data

Internet

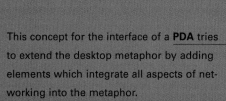

Local area network

Time management

This concept for the interface of a **PDA** tries to extend the desktop metaphor by adding elements which integrate all aspects of networking into the metaphor.
The desktop is situated in a room, and the user can go from this room into other rooms or on to the street.

Personal Digital Assistant

MagicCap
Software for the PC.

Spatial metaphors

The human spatial memory is able to recover information on the basis of the place where it was stored. In the real world this particularly works so well because it involves a movement of the body, the physical action of grasping. But this sense of orientation also seems to work in a virtual environment, in spite of the abstraction. Integrating functions into spatial metaphors is a technique which is often used on the Internet.

Spatial concepts are even used in our language to describe abstract processes, e.g. basis, level, foreground, foundation. The difficulty of spatial metaphors lies in the logical integration of all levels of the hierarchy. The spatial metaphor is generally used for the main level, but the presentation then changes to two dimensions when a menu item is being selected because the content is almost always available in a traditional graphic form.

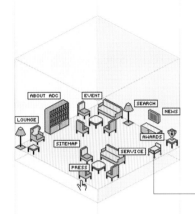

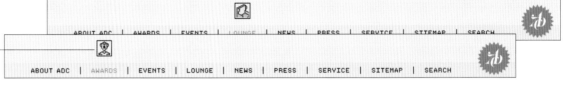

www.adc.de
Website of the German Art Director's Club ADC. All functions of the site are allocated to objects in a room. In the following levels, there is merely a snapshot of the selected object to refer to the introductory navigation, and the basic navigation is implemented with a menu bar.

www.allegra.de
On-line forum of the women's magazine of the same name. A schematic representation of a house serves to connect various chats.

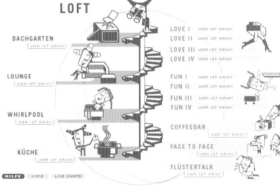

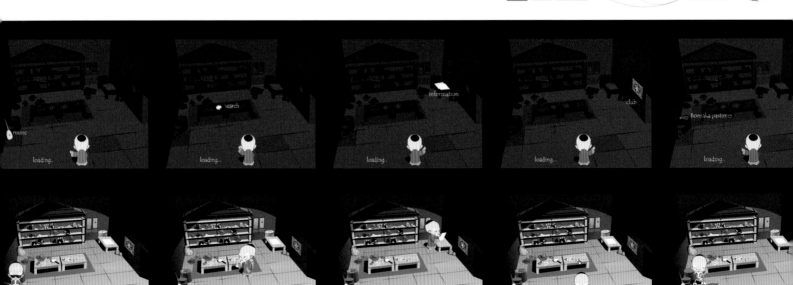

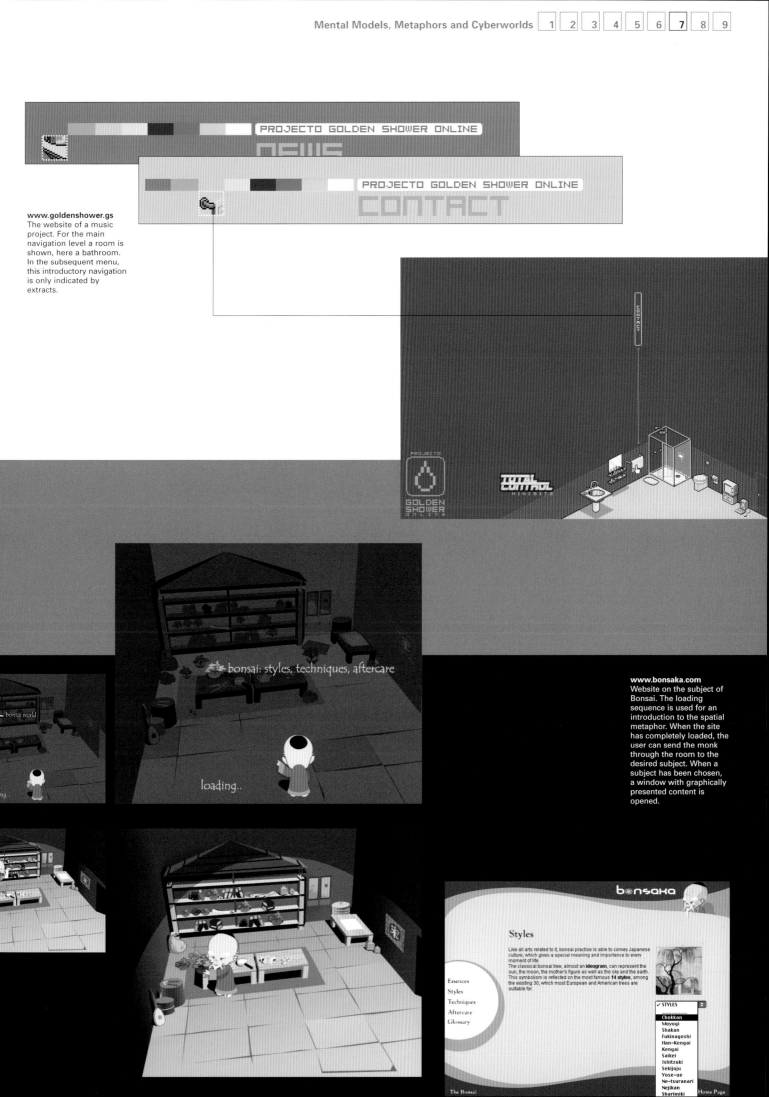

www.goldenshower.gs
The website of a music project. For the main navigation level a room is shown, here a bathroom. In the subsequent menu, this introductory navigation is only indicated by extracts.

www.bonsaka.com
Website on the subject of Bonsai. The loading sequence is used for an introduction to the spatial metaphor. When the site has completely loaded, the user can send the monk through the room to the desired subject. When a subject has been chosen, a window with graphically presented content is opened.

Anthropomorphic beings and avatars

Another way to simplify navigation is to introduce a digital companion who can answer the user's questions. This personification of the services aims to give the user the confidence that he is not alone. Creating figures which either act as a guide to the website or help with questions can often lead to misunderstandings: the capabilities of the system are often overestimated because of the realistic presentation of the figure. The quasi-intelligent reactions of the figure stand and fall with the number of keywords which are stored and which the system can interpret.

And the user's relationship to the character is subject to the same factors as in the real world, i.e. liking and disliking.

Another concept is the creation of an **avatar** which enters the virtual world in place of the user. This technique is very popular in games, and is being increasingly used in e-commerce applications. It permits trial activities, e.g. when used in mail-order clothes stores. But the technology is not yet sophisticated enough and the design grid is too coarse, so this technique has usually lead to unintended laughter.

In Hinduism, avatars are reincarnated beings which descend to the earth. In the computer age, avatars are innovative identities or game figures which the user can take on after entering the virtual world. The term was applied to computers in the early 1980s when programers in the US forces were looking for a term to use for the human artefacts in their simulation games.

ww.bonzi.com
Representation of a search engine based on agents.

www.askjeeves.com
Search engine with full-text search.

Tamagochi
("beloved egg")
A good example of trial actions. In this simple pocket computer game, the user breeds a virtual chick which assumes various forms and personalities depending on the care given.
A sales hit in 1996.

Microsoft Office 2000
Help function in the word processor Microsoft Word.

Playstation: Tombraider
The figure of Lara Croft has acquired a cult status.

www.boo.com
Website of an on-line fashion mail-order company. The figure of Miss Boo gives hints and guides the user through the range of products.

"An agent would be a 'soft robot' living and doing its business within the computer's world."
Alan Kay, 1984

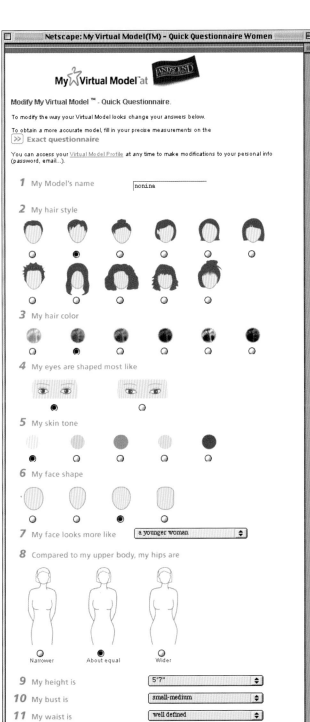

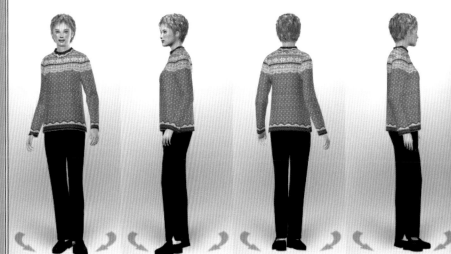

Avatars in virtual worlds

Three-dimensional worlds have so far mainly been used in the entertainment sector, e.g. for chats. In such systems, all users are represented by avatars. To participate in this type of chat, the user must create a figure that represents them. The anonymity enables and encourages participants to create an avatar that has characteristics which are completely different from its creator.

By contrast with sites which use a spatial metaphor merely as an introduction to all areas of the content, in these applications the room is the framework within which the various participants can move and act. The action does not follow a plan, it results from the actions of the participants and they can all follow it in real time. To guarantee intuitive navigation, the metaphor is closely modelled on reality.

www.habbohotel.com
The website of a virtual hotel which, like a real hotel, offers innumerable rooms in which users can make contact with people. The isometric perspective of the display enables the users to find their bearings. The users can move between the rooms by using a navigator in the form of a list. This "hyper-real" movement helps the users not to get lost.

"On-line, no one knows you're a dog. Or a male. Or a 13-year-old girl."
Dorion Sagan

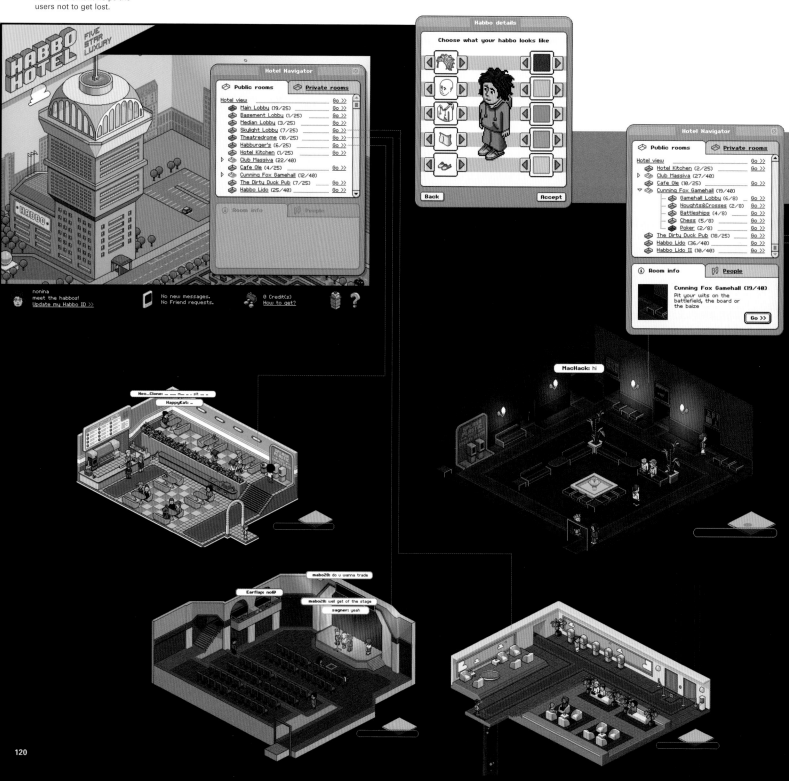

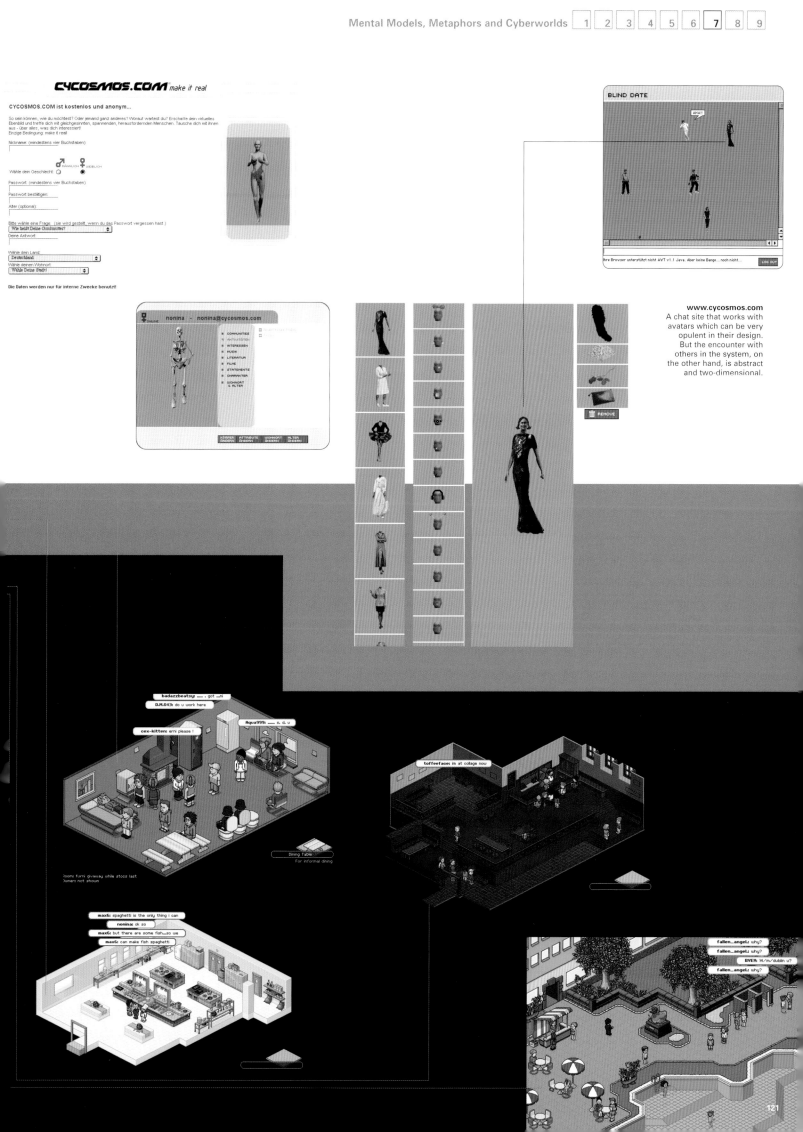

www.cycosmos.com
A chat site that works with
avatars which can be very
opulent in their design.
But the encounter with
others in the system, on
the other hand, is abstract
and two-dimensional.

Disorientation as a concept

The deliberate disorientation of the player is only part of the concept in game applications. Making navigation difficult because the user does not have a full overview is a main element of most adventure, first person and shooter games. Physical feedback and spatial memory do not apply because the user does not really move, so orientation is deliberately difficult in such applications, and this is part of the attraction of the game.

Here we can see that the third dimension does not always improve the orientation of the user, especially when it is displayed on a two-dimensional screen.

Another prime area of application is in simulations. For example, situations which would be dangerous or expensive in the real world can be moved into **cyberspace**.

The term "cyberspace" was first used by William Gibson in his science fiction "Neuromancer" of 1984.

Counterstrike
Sierra

Soldier of Fortune 1
Raven Software

Dungeon Siege
Microsoft

St. Maarten 2001
Microsoft FlightSimulator
2000 / PRO

Hong Kong Kai Tak 2000
Microsoft FlightSimulator
2000 / PRO

Soldier of Fortune 2
Double Helix
Raven Software

"While the interfaces evolve, the software will move beyond violent games to business gaming, problem solving and decision-making, vicarious travel, and ultimately to flying through information – perhaps all human knowledge."
Richard Saul Wurman

Doom/Quake
id Software

Virtual reality

Another type of virtual reality is the documentation of physical locations with the aid of navigable **panoramic images**. In this way it is possible to visit faraway or inaccessible places and gain a very vivid impression of them. This technique has become established for visits to museums, advance orders for theatre tickets and bookings for hotels and conference rooms.

The optical distortion superimposed on the image cut-out is surprisingly similar to human perception. In a further step, individual locations can be combined into virtual "walks" with several stopping points, thus creating tours of exhibitions and cities.

www.sydneyoperahouse.com
A virtual visit to the opera house in Sydney. A model created in the computer can be sub-divided into four levels, thus offering a navigation model in which the user can jump to individual positions.

Kempinski Hotels Germany
Multimedia CD-Rom to facilitate bookings for banquet and conference rooms in the Kempinski Hotels in Germany. The rooms can be arranged with various seating patterns on a trial basis and then reviewed.

"The computer is something that can recreate that experience and a thousand others without having a rich father. We can transport ourselves today in a fashion that no king of ancient times could ever do, and we don't have to be a king."
Alan Kay

Virtual objects

The presentation of three-dimensional objects on the Internet has not yet become widespread – largely for technical reasons. However, three-dimensional presentations offer a very intuitive navigation which provides much more information than a photograph. Information is displayed directly on the object, so different versions, e.g. colours, can be tried out on the object.

The user controls the operation directly with the mouse. The three-dimensional movement of the object is linked to the two-dimensional movement of the cursor. The user can "grasp" the object and look at it from all sides.

www.3danywhere.com
A supplier of software to place navigable 3D objects on the Internet. Shown here with a rendering of a car.

The Aeron Chair
Multimedia product information designed by the company Studio Archetype for Herman Miller Inc. According to Clement Mok it was "the most monotonous photo session ever", consisting of 1512 individual pictures.

www.3danywhere.com
The glasses shown here are more suited to this technique because they do not need to be scaled down so much.

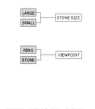

www.3danywhere.com
Smaller objects which are displayed on screen at a scale of 1:1 seem to work well: the ring can be visualised in various materials, and it is even possible to test a personal engraving.

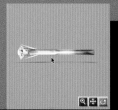

Navigable films prepared photographically or from CAD data must be distinguished from three-dimensional data calculated in real time. The former require far more technical preparation, and the latter often suffer from a lack of detail which makes the object appear sterile.

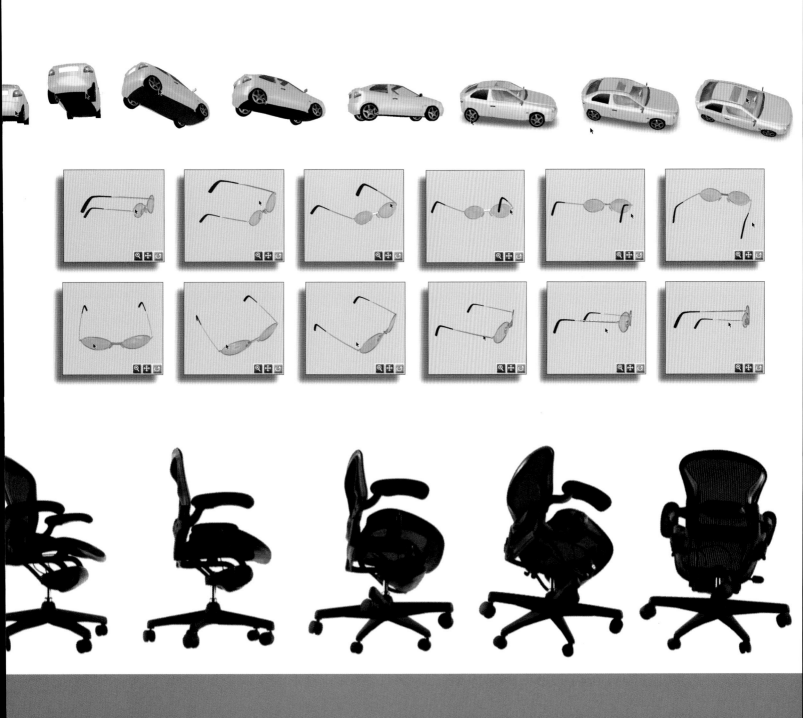

New Frontiers

1 2 3 4 5 6 7 **8** 9

Sep.2000

Nov.2000

This chapter brings together websites that really make full use of the medium and thus set new standards. In addition to innovative and experimental sites which try out new navigation and interaction techniques, the chapter provides an overview of the formal and aesthetic possibilities which are available in this medium and shows examples in which familiar and stereotypical navigation elements and symbols have been developed one step further. A collection of playful and experimental websites which explore the interaction of visual and auditive elements rounds off this overview.

Experimental navigation

The size of the screen and the wealth of information to be presented will always be in a state of tension. Attempts to find new ways to process information for the medium and make it accessible through good navigation are therefore all the more important. Continuity is an important factor for orientation.

Many experiments explore the potential of animation and morphing techniques for the creation of flowing movements within fields of information, and thus search for new concepts to preserve the information context.

www.relevare.com
Website of the company of the same name. The zoom is used as the navigation element. The four quadrants represent the main categories of the site. The user clicks to zoom into the individual areas. The zoomed path is shown at the bottom edge as an extra navigation bar.

www.uncontrol.com
A website which provides open source files in Flash which anyone can download. The projects are represented by individual squares. Those that have already been seen are linked by a thread in the corresponding order.

www.automat.at
The website of the media agency of the same name. Navigation follows a simple principle: each additional information level is folded open as an add-on, so the visitor always knows where he or she has come from.

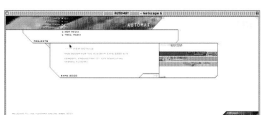

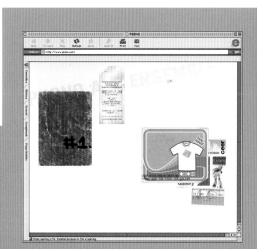

www.phono.com
The portfolio of the media agency of the same name. Fragments spread around the screen can be moved freely and give small clues which reveal more about the agency represented.

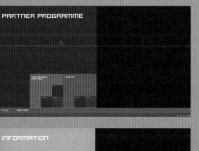

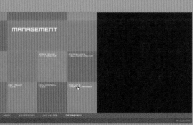
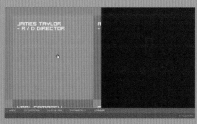

Latest (can go no farther!)
only 582 days left!
Steve Dietz (steve.dietz@walkerart.org)
2002.Feb.17

Moment in time:
Fitness in Wartime
Jordan Crandall (crandall@blast.org)
2001.Dec.18

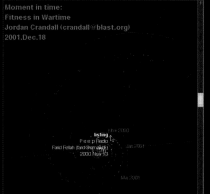
Reading:
IBAM New Media launches Under_score
Wayne Ashley (washley@bam.org)
2001.Oct.24

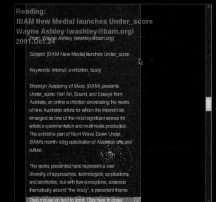

www.rhizome.org
An experimental time line of an on-line forum. The time line spirals down to the bottom of the screen and can be navigated at different speeds by using a vertical slide.

The Web as a playground and digital sandbox

Websites by media designers act as a playground and demonstration object to move development forward. The Internet as a medium lends a dynamic dimension to the global exchange of ideas and experience.

www.etnies-germany.com
The first navigation level of an on-line catalogue for sportswear. Clicking on the direction arrows loads the corresponding menu.

www.futurefarmers.com
This site is a forum for various media projects – including the site "They rule" – which visualise the economic links between large American corporations.

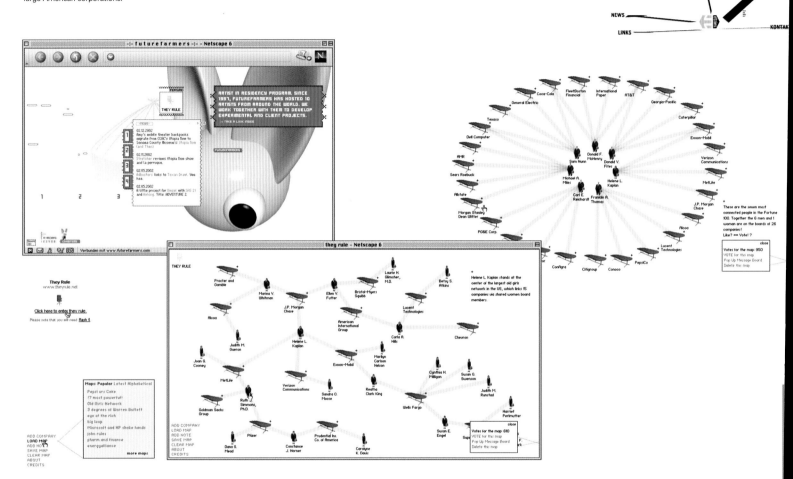

www.orisinal.com
A collection of on-line games which explore new navigation possibilities.

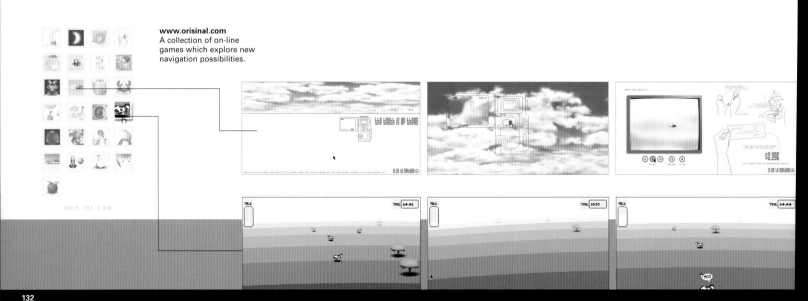

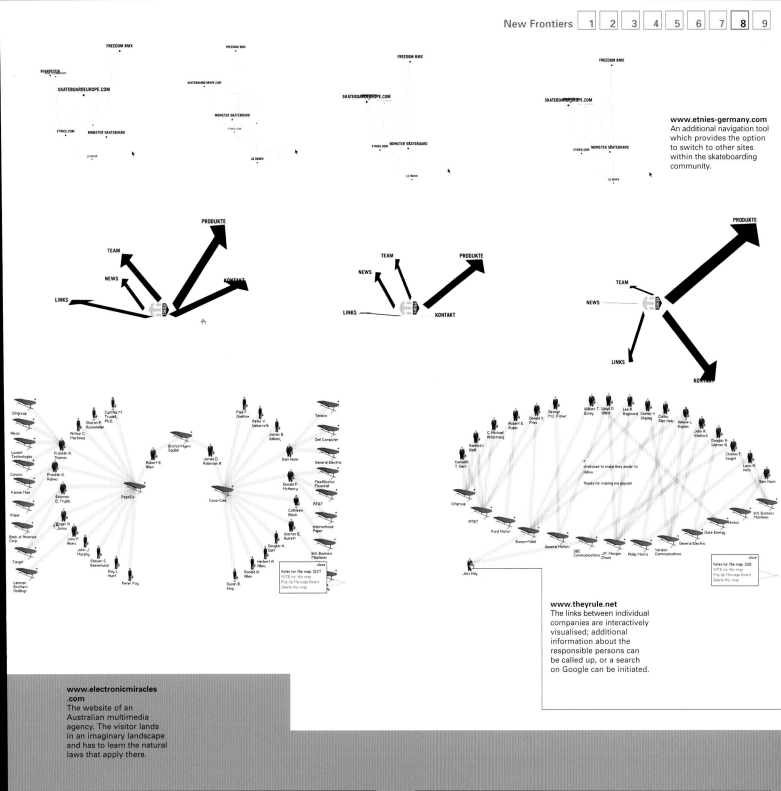

www.etnies-germany.com
An additional navigation tool which provides the option to switch to other sites within the skateboarding community.

www.theyrule.net
The links between individual companies are interactively visualised; additional information about the responsible persons can be called up, or a search on Google can be initiated.

www.electronicmiracles .com
The website of an Australian multimedia agency. The visitor lands in an imaginary landscape and has to learn the natural laws that apply there.

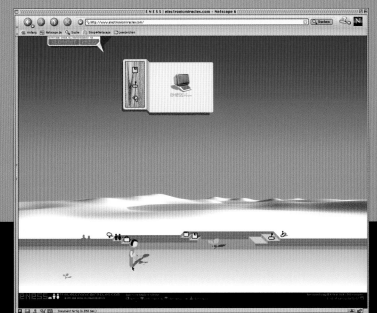

Virtual physics

A number of websites deal experimentally with the specific features of the Web and the available tools. A program that is often used for experimental sites is Macromedia Flash. With its vector-based structure it is fast, and by extending the scripting functions it can become a powerful programing environment. Applications created with this program can integrate sophisticated graphics and interact smoothly with the computer.

Among other tasks, it is used to simulate physical laws such as gravity, mass inertia and elasticity. The interaction with the computer is thus enriched by a component which can be experienced almost physically. The insights from these experiments are used in the design of navigation elements.

www.yugop.com
Kiriya.com
One of the most influential websites dealing with virtual physics on the Internet.

www.praystation.com
A website with an extensive collection of open source experiments. The illustration shows a simulation of bacteria growth.

www.uncontrol.com
Torch
Another collection which simulates scientific phenomena mathematically.

www.yugop.com
elastic body 01

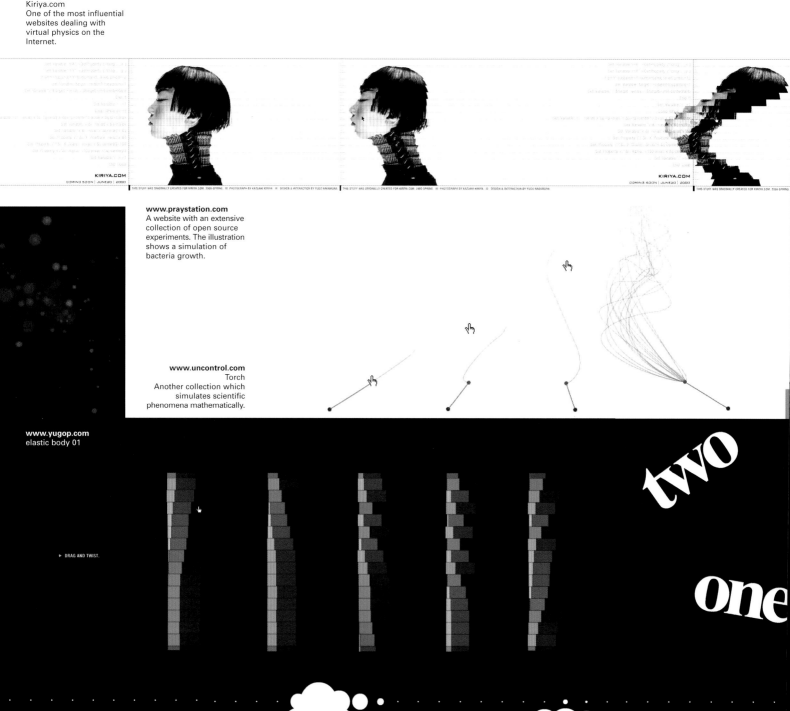

In this way, for example, scroll bars can be
created with a slide control that can be set
in motion with a strong "push" and will then
continue to move until it reaches the end,
like in the physical world.

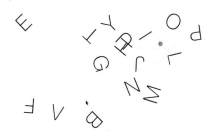
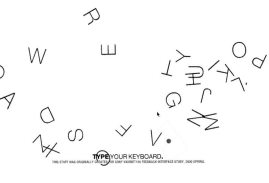

TYPEYOUR KEYBOARD.
THIS STUFF WAS ORIGINALLY CREATED FOR SONY VAIONET100 FEEDBACK INTERFACE STUDY, 2000 SPRING.

www.yugop.com
vaionet100-study

www.levitated.net
Double Helix Expansion
Buttons
A homage to digital artists
such as John Maeda, this
site showcases the beauty
of data-structures,
algorithms and logic in the
context of design and
interaction.
This site provides clear
and concise explanations
of how each of the many
pieces work as well as all
the source files.

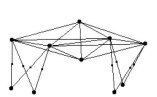
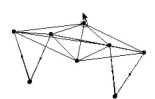

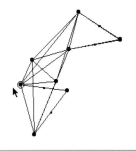

www.yugop.com
rigid body 01

one
two

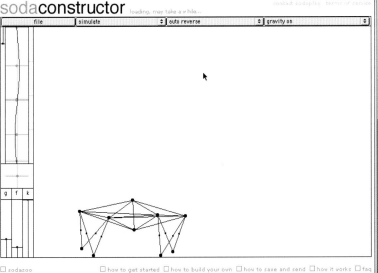

**www.sodaplay.com/
constructor**
A construction program
that can be used to create
link chains. These objects
can then be set in motion
under various atmospheric
conditions, e.g. subject
to gravity.

www.yugop.com
year of the snake

Every medium develops its own visual language in conjunction with the tools used. But the medium can only develop its own identity when it has left the imitation of other media behind it.

A good sign: hand-made paper backgrounds and other relics from the world of paper are dying out on the Internet. The medium is beginning to reflect on itself.

Typical design elements of the computer interface are being reinterpreted, the first waves of retrospective treatment are beginning. Most navigation elements can be assumed to be familiar in their function, so they can be abstracted or distorted accordingly. In fact, there is now even competition in the **reduction** of design elements, and every pixel is fought for.

www.futurefarmer.com

www.db-db.com

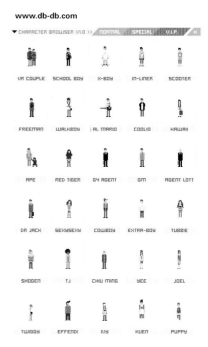

www.vectorize.de

www.arkndesign.com

www.flipflopflyin.com

see also pages 110|111

SILKSCREEN
ABCDEFGHIJKLMNOPQRSTUVWXYZ

MINI 7
ABCDEFGHIJKLMNOPQRSTUVWXYZ

Silkscreen, Mini 7
Specifically designed
screen fonts. Since they
are minimised in height,
only capitals are
available.
Due to their size these
typefaces are particularly
suited to label navigation
elements.

www.afterlab.com

www.aeriform.co.uk

www.wireframe.com

www.pixelsurgeon.com

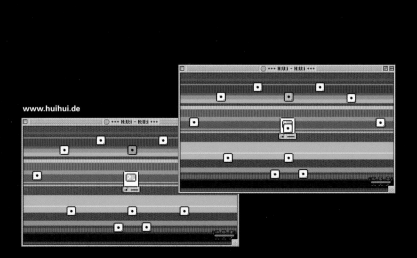

www.huihui.de

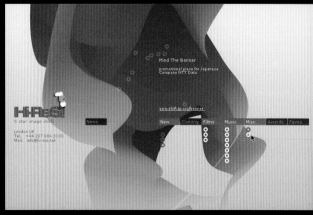

www.hi-res.net

Exploring the auditive dimension of multimedia

Real multimedia experience requires auditive elements. In the interactive medium, however, the focus is not so much on musical accompaniments. Instead, the sound channel is used for a more intensive expression of the interaction between the user and the computer by confirming the user's actions with auditive **feedback**.

This response by the system provides guidance to the visitor and makes navigation easier. The significance of the sound channel for navigation will increase as computers of all operating systems acquire "multimedia capability".

see also pages 32|33

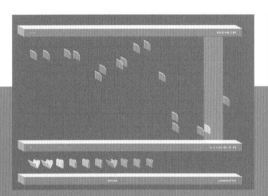
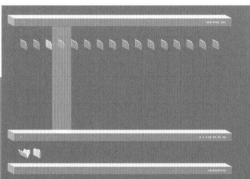
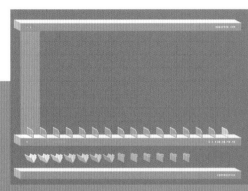

www.modifyme.com
Experimental synthesiser.

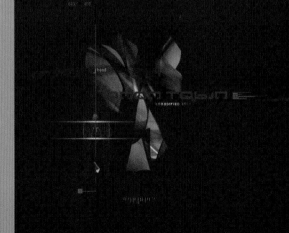

www.amontobin.com
The website of an electronic music artist; the user can explore an interactive world of sound.

www.djvadim.com
Experimental mixer. On the areas at the sides there are sounds, scratches and beats that react to mouse clicks and can be looped.

The warning sounds given by operating
systems and programs represent a minimum
standard which is easy to surpass.
Experimental sites integrate the user
auditively by responding to his actions with
changes in volume, pitch, tone, stereo and
echo effects.

www.suba.com.br
Interactive sound
environments.

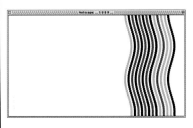
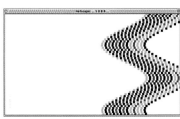
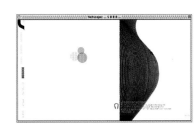

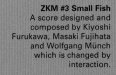

ZKM #3 Small Fish
A score designed and
composed by Kiyoshi
Furukawa, Masaki Fujihata
and Wolfgang Münch
which is changed by
interaction.

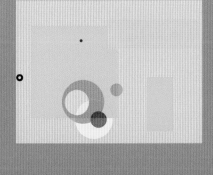
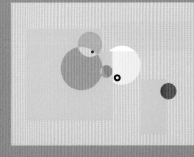
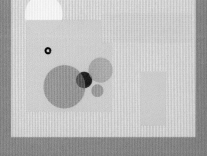

Medium-specific experiments

Direct interaction with other people on the Internet is still in its infancy. Apart from multi-player games such as Doom, such interaction is restricted to the exchange of texts in chat rooms. Here, too, sites which are initially experimental in character can provide new impetus.

http://tate.cix.co.uk
Interactive implementation of the famous Warhol quotation: "A time will come when everybody is famous for five minutes." Every visitor can upload a photograph to the site, and this photo is shown on the website for various minutes with the typical Warhol distortions.

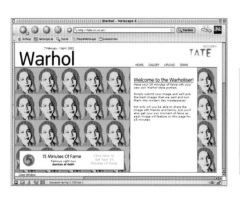

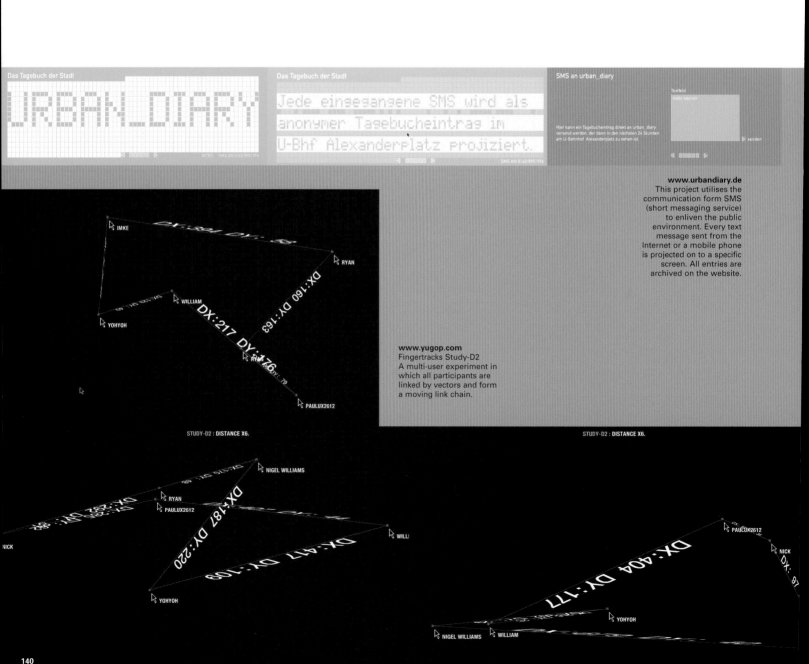

www.urbandiary.de
This project utilises the communication form SMS (short messaging service) to enliven the public environment. Every text message sent from the Internet or a mobile phone is projected on to a specific screen. All entries are archived on the website.

www.yugop.com
Fingertracks Study-D2
A multi-user experiment in which all participants are linked by vectors and form a moving link chain.

Other factors which are distinctively characteristic of this digital, interactive medium include a stronger use of randomness, time and personalisation. Randomness: the site can have a different look every time it is visited. Time: the site can react differently at different times of the day. Personalisation: the site "knows" who is visiting it and can draw intelligent conclusions.

The linking of different input and output channels is increasingly being used. Websites to send SMS messages and websites that display SMS messages already exist. Here, too, experimental installations show what cross-over concepts the future is likely to bring.

www.blinkenlights.de
Experimental installation of the Chaos Computer Club; simple animations can be generated with the aid of a small program. The "output medium" is the facade of a building in Berlin.

STUDY-D2 : DISTANCE X6.

The next level of Web culture

The nearest branch can
be determined by a zoom
sequence.

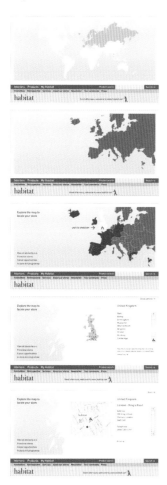

The next step in the development of the
Internet is to agree on a visually rich design
suited to the media which is easy to maintain
and update. In view of the fact that there are
not many viable economic models on the
Internet at present, many companies are
hesitant in taking this step.

On the one hand there are ambitious websites
by media designers and agencies, and on
the other hand there are rationally designed
web presentations which keep to a simple,
highly text-based standard which allows
updating to be automated by using editorial
systems. There are just a few dynamically
generated and visually oriented sites that
show what is possible.

Entertaining load sequen-
ces supported by anima-
tions show the user that
the connection is still active.

The medium is used well
in the presentation of the
information, which
successfully combines static product illustrations
with superimposed
animation sequences.

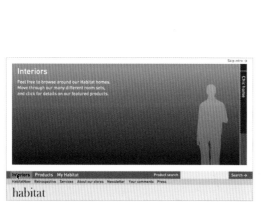

www.habitat.net
An interactive on-line
catalogue of the English
furnishing chain habitat.

The time of day is taken
into account in the welcome
that is given.

habitat   Good morning, welcome to www.habitat.net   Good afternoon, welcome to www.habitat.net   Good evening, welcome to www.habitat.net

142

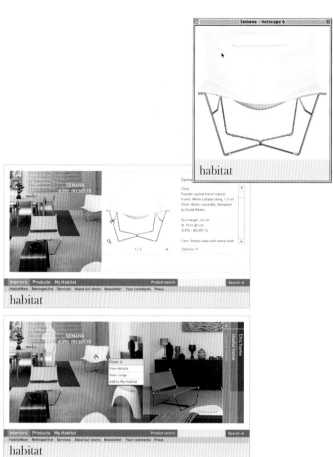

The company history is shown in the form of a time line.

The products are represented by thumbnails. This is easier to use than a list of the product names.

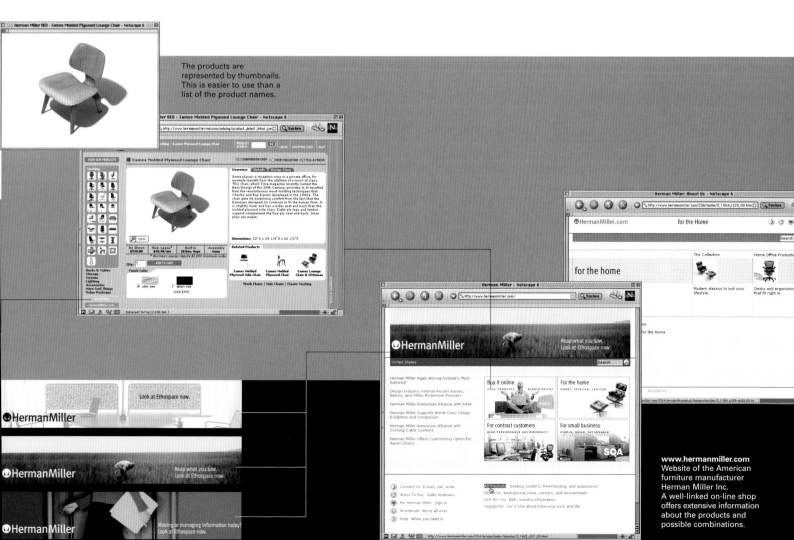

www.hermanmiller.com
Website of the American furniture manufacturer Herman Miller Inc. A well-linked on-line shop offers extensive information about the products and possible combinations.

What´s Next?

1 2 3 4 5 6 7 8 9

The Internet goes mobile. An increasing number of computers are linked to the Internet by radio communication.
In addition to the advantages of no longer needing cables at home or in the office, this development offers prospects of a new basic access to information in the public environment. A number of universities, airports and even city centres are now equipped with radio relay networks.
A laptop with the appropriate network card can go on-line directly without any additional configuration in these locations. This type of mobile use will change the services offered, the way they are presented and the means used for navigation.

Mobile Internet creates a conflict between the optimum presentation of the information and the feasible size of mobile devices. Technically, the output devices could become smaller and lighter, but the anthropometric reference dimensions do not change. For the so-called "babyfaces", i.e. the smaller screens, the information needs to be broken down differently. The designer must fight for every **pixel**.

And even though these screens will be in full colour in the foreseeable future, the available space is still comparatively small. It must also be taken into account that the possible situations for use will be far more heterogeneous than they are for the carefully placed computer screen at home or in the office.

see also pages 136|137

http://mobile.tomorrow.de
A mobile Internet service that has been optimised for pocket PCs. The established convention of using tabs for navigation was used for this format.

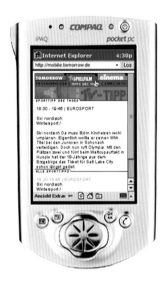

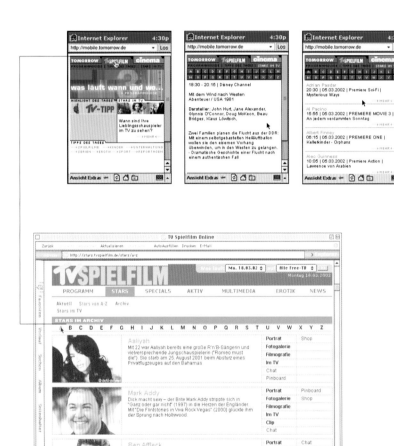

Deutsche Bahn WAP service
A version of the Deutsche Bahn Internet site for mobile display via wireless application protocol (WAP). The navigation uses scrollable lists of menu items.

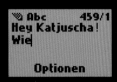

SMS (**S**hort **M**essaging **S**ervice), a successful mobile phone service in which text messages with a maximum of 160 characters are sent from one mobile phone to another and from the Internet to a mobile phone.

This forces people to use brief language and abbreviations such as CU (see you). Successors such as **E**nhanced **M**essaging **S**ervice and **M**ultimedia **M**essaging **S**ervice will also enable video and audio sequences to be transmitted.

An additional challenge for the designer is to scale down the network resources for these different output situations. Whether a website is used "on the road" on a palmtop or at home on a computer screen, it needs to have a high recognition value and consistent navigation.

On the software side, scripting languages such as XML (e**X**tensible **M**arkup **L**anguage) offer the possibility to break up the content through different output masks depending on the output device used.

www.cinema.de

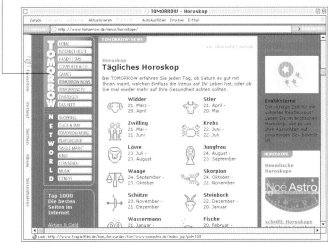

www.tomorrow.de

i-mode is a standard developed for mobile phones with colour display, similar to WAP. It was introduced in Japan in 1999, and its success is due to the combination of cell broadcasting and interactive WAP; i-mode appliances are always on-line.
Applications: on-line games, e-mail, and content services ranging from daily news to dating/chatting. Display size: 120x160 px.

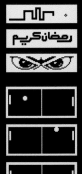

www.Jamba.de
Supplier of dial tones, operator logos and games for mobile phones.

The form of interaction is changing

The development of practicable forms of interaction with small mobile computers is fully under way. A number of forms have arisen. In addition to the smaller and smaller notebooks equipped with a full **miniature keyboard** and a joystick which offer conventional interaction, PDAs offer **pen tool input** and handwriting recognition, with various navigation pads and **direction keys** for navigation.

As with the design of the visual interface, the fact that it may be necessary in some situations to operate the device with one hand plays a significant role here, too.

Pocket PCs
Nokia 9210 Communicator
Entries are made by keyboard and navigation pad. Two-handed control is necessary.

Mobile telephone
Nokia 3330 WAP
At a size of 84x49 px, about 64 characters fit on a mobile phone display. The user already needs to scroll for an SMS with 120 characters; this is done with the hardware arrow keys. Control is possible with one hand.

PDA
Handspring Visor
Personal **D**igital **A**ssistant with a pressure-sensitive display. Entries are made with a pen tool and two-handed control is necessary.

www.sodaplay.com
Migration of the on-line construction game "Soda Constructor" to mobile phone format. The different hardware platform requires new forms of interaction with the familiar software. (software prototype)

Windows CE
Migration of the Microsoft operating system for pocket PCs.

This illustration shows the transfer time needed for one Megabyte of data using different types of mobile communication networks.
(unit = one second)

Wireless Hand PC
NEXiO S150 by Samsung
A device with a range of functions similar to a desktop computer. Display size: 800x480 px.

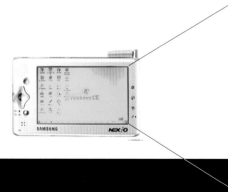

GSM
Global **S**ystem for **M**obile communication

HSCD/GPRS
High **S**peed **C**ircuit **S**witched **D**ata/**G**eneral **P**acket **R**adio **S**ervice
(varying transmission rates)

UMTS
Universal **M**obile **T**elecommunications **S**ervice

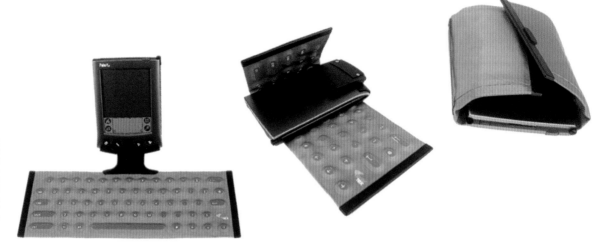

PalmPilot/elektex.com
For navigation with the pen tool, the user must learn a new type of handwriting which the computer can interpret. If users find that too complicated, they can connect a (flexible) keyboard.

You have a call from:
Jack
in his car
Talk Now
Take Message

mob-i Smartphone
www.AMandA.com
Software simulation for the handling, services and operation of a smartphone by AMandA for Samsung. Areas of application: relationships, self-enhancement, information resources, entertainment and mobile e-commerce, e.g. driving assistance, smart yellow pages, and e-coupons, implemented in Macromedia Flash.

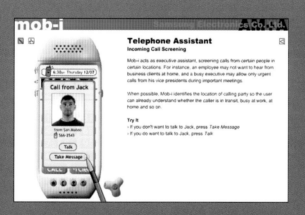

Pawgo.com
Internet portal for the Palm for topics such as news, finance, sports etc. Display size: 160x160 px.

mobile.yahoo.com
Internet portal for the Palm with messages and search engine. Display size: 160x160 px.

Palm OS Organiser
Calendar for the Palm.

i-Disk
www.x-drive.com
www.freedrive.com
The term "hotelling" stands for the opposite strategy to Internet providers which offer hard disk space on the Internet. Based on the assumption that computers are available almost everywhere, the user no longer carries his own device about. Instead, he can log on to any computer and work on his own personal desktop. This enables the range of functions of mobile appliances to be reduced, they no longer have to perform every task.

Local hard disk

Web space

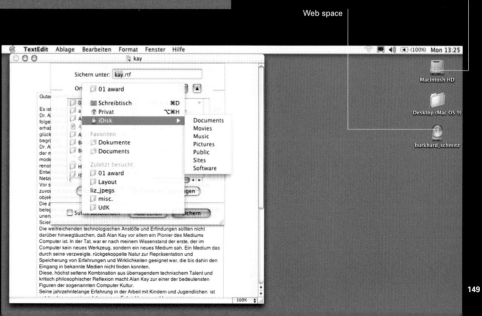

The network knows where the user is and adapts the content to this location.

Locating the surfer will be another component which will play a role for Internet navigation in particular. Here, the user is the navigator: as he or she moves through the real world, the Web content is adjusted depending on the user´s position.

The Internet becomes a meta-level of information that is superimposed on reality. The user can call up additional information from any physical location. The mobile device becomes a digital divining rod. The navigation structure within the information is developed from the parameter of the location, all other parameters are subordinated.

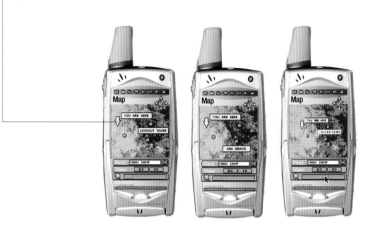

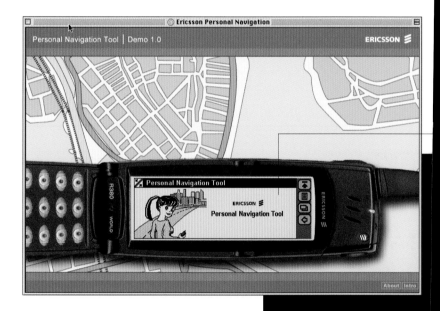

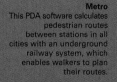

Metro
This PDA software calculates pedestrian routes between stations in all cities with an underground railway system, which enables walkers to plan their routes.

FireViewer
This software enables large colour pictures to be panned on a PDA.

Citikey London
On-line city guide for hand-held PCs.

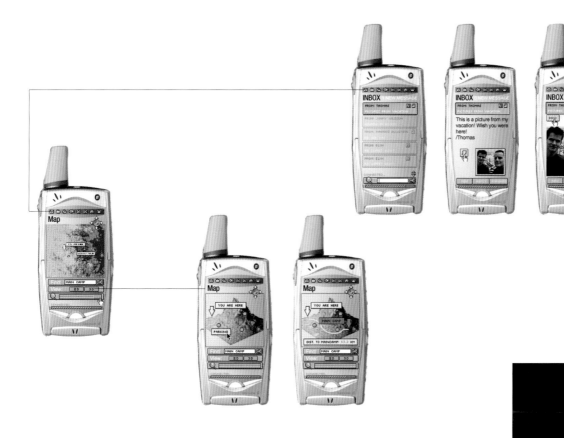

www.ericsson.com/
mobileinternet/intouch.htm
Study on a location-based
service. Identification of
the user's present position
means that services such
as 2D and 3D visualisation
of the direct surrounds are
possible. The user can call
up topographic information
and infrastructure details.

www.ericsson.com/
mobileinternet/offerings/
personalnavigation.html
Simulated navigation
software for the interface
of the Ericsson R 380e.
The extreme landscape
format of the display
permits a good display for
body text such as navigation
paths. In the display of
graphics such as town
plans, the user must
scroll immediately.

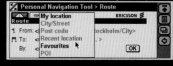

Intelligent products

Networking can take many forms. It is not always obvious and does not always need to be initiated explicitly by dialling in. Work is being carried out on the networking of buildings, cars and items of clothing. This form of integration of new technology into the man-made environment is also known as "ubiquitous computing". Objects which appear "normal" acquire a planning and logistic dimension through networking. For example, the intelligent refrigerator at home can order replacements for its content on its own initiative. The car can make itself an appointment in the repair workshop if it notices a malfunction.

Many of these routines are carried out independently without any need for the user to deal with an interface. The integration of these systems into traditional products will be linked to the traditional use of these products. This makes operation easier.

www.media.mit.edu/ttt
The "things that think" project at the MEDIA Lab of the MIT (Massachusetts Institute of Technology) has been working since 1991 on the integration of computer-aided systems into the man-made environment.

Philips Design
New Nomads,
an exploration of Wearable
Electronics: **Imaginair**

The air hostess' uniform incorporates a personal digital assistant with flexible LCD screen, a wireless earpiece and a microphone – which the hostess can use to communicate with the cabin crew whilst she is serving the passengers.

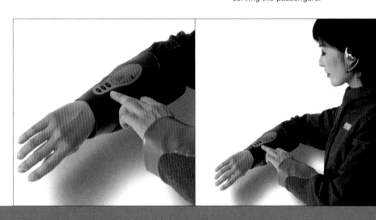

152

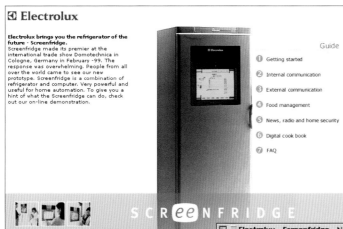

Electrolux

Electrolux brings you the refrigerator of the future - Screenfridge.
Screenfridge made its premier at the international trade show Domotechnica in Cologne, Germany in February -99. The response was overwhelming. People from all over the world came to see our new prototype. Screenfridge is a combination of refrigerator and computer. Very powerful and useful for home automation. To give you a hint of what the Screenfridge can do, check out our on-line demonstration.

Guide
1 Getting started
2 Internal communication
3 External communication
4 Food management
5 News, radio and home security
6 Digital cook book
7 FAQ

SCReeNFRIDGE

www.electrolux.se/
screenfridge/
The refrigerator as a communication centre in the household.
An intelligent device with a touchscreen and Internet browser. Range of functions: radio and TV, video messages, cookery book.

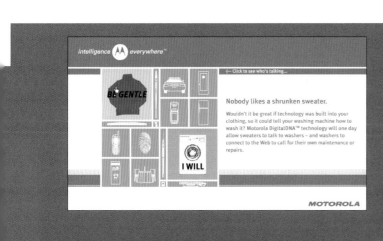

intelligence everywhere™

BE GENTLE

I WILL

←·· Click to see who's talking...

Nobody likes a shrunken sweater.

Wouldn't it be great if technology was built into your clothing, so it could tell your washing machine how to wash it? Motorola DigitalDNA™ technology will one day allow sweaters to talk to washers – and washers to connect to the Web to call for their own maintenance or repairs.

MOTOROLA

I'M LOST

I'LL FIND YOU

I'M EMPTY

I'M CHEAP

www.motorola.com
Visualisation of digital DNA technology by Motorola which is being used to develop the networking and communication between objects.

wear
Cooperation project between MIT and the design company IDEO on the subject of wearable computers. Scenarios based on two different user profiles aim to design and develop the appropriate hardware components.

wear
MIT+IDEO
project overview   scenario one   scenario two
Kio   Guy

Guy's Base Unit ←

related sites
MIT
BMW
IDEO

My base unit contains the central processor, memory, short/long range wireless communications and power unit to keep my system running. It is very slim and lightweight. Although I have friends who prefer the completely "soft" vest version, I use the belt-mounted version because it fits more with my sartorial preferences. I don't even think about "wearing" my computer anymore, it's gotten to be as natural as wearing a watch, (which, by the way, I no longer do). I imagine that the next step will be having my computer become a part of my body.

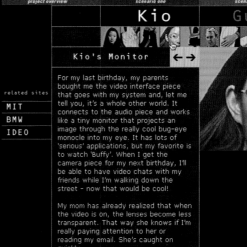

wear
MIT+IDEO
project overview   scenario one   scenario two
Kio   Guy

Kio's Monitor ←→

related sites
MIT
BMW
IDEO

For my last birthday, my parents bought me the video interface piece that goes with my system and, let me tell you, it's a whole other world. It connects to the audio piece and works like a tiny monitor that projects an image through the really cool bug-eye monocle into my eye. It has lots of 'serious' applications, but my favorite is to watch 'Buffy'. When I get the camera piece for my next birthday, I'll be able to have video chats with my friends while I'm walking down the street - now that would be cool!

My mom has already realized that when the video is on, the lenses become less transparent. That way she knows if I'm really paying attention to her or reading my email. She's caught on quickly.

Sources

Alexander, Ishikawa, Silverstein, Jacobson, Fiksdahl-King, Angel. **A Pattern Language.** Oxford. 1977

Bartram, Ho, Dill and Henigman. **The Continous Zoom: A Constrained Fisheye Technique for Viewing and Navigating Large Information Spaces.** Graphics and Multimedia Research Laboratory, Center for systems Science, Simon Fraser University. 1995

Brand, Stewart. **The Media Lab.** Penguin Books. 1988

Buckminster Fuller, R. **Your Private Sky.** Lars Müller Publishers. 1999

Conklin, Jeff. **"Hypertext: An Introduction and Survey".** IEEE Computer. 1987

Davis, Jordan, Singe and Baumann. **New Masters of Flash.** Friends of Ed. 2000

Dodge und Kitchin. **Atlas of Cyberspace.** Addison Wesley. 2001

Dyson, Esther. **Release 2.0.** Viking. 1997

pages 56l57, 58l59, 110l111
www.12go.de
www.absolut.com
www.adidas.com
www.americanhistory.si.edu/house/families/choates.asp
www.amoeba.com.sg
www.apple.com
www.archpark.org.il
www.artofarchitect.com
www.ashwhite.com
www.automat.at
www.benetton.com/colors
www.bmu.de
www.camper.com
www.dreamworks.com
www.duden.de
www.duesseldorf.de
www.eneri.net
http://fingertips.newdamage.com
www.flashcan.com
www.ford.com
www.form.de
www.fraboom.com
www.honda.com
www.iconmedialab.de
www.i-dmedia.com
www.imstall.com
www.karstadt.de
www.leonce.de
www.lego.com
www.letsbuyit.com
www.lunchboxstudios.com
www.metadesign.com
www.napster.com
www.nasa20.de
www.ninjai.com
www.onceuponaforest.com
www.pentagram.com
http://plane.kalisto.com
www.puma.de
www.quam.de
www.rtl.de
www.rtl2.de
www.shift.com
www.shrek.com
www.smartmoney.com
www.sony.com
www.sonystyle-europe.com
www.starbucks.com
www.tchibo.de
www.tonystone.com
www.ultrashock.com
www.vivatv.de
www.wholetruth.com
www.wireframe.co.za
www.yahoo.com
www.yugop.com
www.zitty.de

pages 34l35
"Homer", Iris and Nina Schnitter, Diploma 2000
"Invitation for scrambled eggs", Michael Grewer,
project 1998

page 38
"eBureau", Imke Pienkos, Diploma 2001

Eames/Morrison. **Powers of Ten.**
Scientific American Library. 1982

Frutiger, Adrian. **Der Mensch und seine
Zeichen.** Fourier. 1978

Gibson, William. **Virtual Light.**
Bantam Books. 1994

Infomation design journal.
Vol. 10, No. 1. 2000/01

Kahn und Lenk. **Mapping Web Sites.**
RotoVision. 2000

Laurel, Brenda. **The Art of Human-Computer
Interface Design.** Addison Wesley. 1990

Maeda and Antonelli. **Design by Numbers.**
MIT Press. 1999

Maeda and Negroponte. **Maeda @ Media.**
Thames and Hudson. 2000

Marcus, Aaron. **Development of a
Future Wireless Information Device.**
AM + A Inc. 2002

McKelvey, Roy. **Hypergraphics.**
RotoVision SA. 1998

McLuhan/Fiore. **The Medium is the
Message.** HardWired. 1967

McLuhan, Marshall. **Understanding Media.**
Fundus. 1964

Minsky, Marvin. **The Society of Mind.**
Touchstone Simon and Schuster. 1985/1986

Mok, Clement. **Designing Business.**
Adobe Press California. 1996

Negroponte, Nicholas. **Being Digital.**
Verlag Alfred A. Knopf NY. 1995

Neuhart, Neuhart und Eames.
Eames Design. Ernst + Sohn. 1989

Norman, Donald A. **The Design of Everyday
Things.** Currency Doubleday. 1988

Popcorn, Faith. **The Popcorn Report.**
Doubleday. 1991

Smolan and Erwitt. **One Digital Day.**
Times book. 1998

Tufte, Edward R. **Visual Explanations.**
Graphic Press. 1997

Tufte, Edward R. **Envisioning Information.**
Graphic Press. 1990

Wieners & Pescovitz. **Reality Check.**
HardWired. 1996

Wildbur and Burke. **Information Graphics:
Innovative Solutions in Comtemporary
Design.** Thames and Hudson. 1998

Wurman, Richard Saul. **Information Anxiety 2.**
Que Indianapolis. November 2000

Wurman, Richard Saul. **Information
Architects.** Graphis. 1996

Wurman, Richard Saul. **Understanding.**
Ted Conferences Inc. 1999

Brian Morris: for believing in this project and us.

Veruschka Götz: for navigating us through the world of publishing.

Natalia Price-Cabrera: for patiently but thoroughly checking our material.

Alan Kay: as you can see by the number of his quotes, he is a true inspiration to us.

Hans Nick Roericht: for teaching us that impatience is a virtue.

Heinz Wohner: for being so fast and so easy.

Katrin Richter: for being at the right place at the right time.

Aaron Marcus and Claudia Dallendörfer: for offering their experience to us while being thousands of miles away.

Christine Strothotte: for backing us and being a good listener.

Juliane Rief, Charlotte Kaiser, Alexander Jackert, Carmen Traud: for the bravery of being interns at 7.5 during this project.

Imke Pienkos: for stamina and starting her career with a difficult project.

Studio 7.5: thanks to the whole crew for power-surfing, support and inspiration.

Carola Zwick & Burkhard Schmitz,
March 2002

A

above the fold 101
address 18 21 26 27 86
agent systems 85
alias 115
animation 130
anonymity 120
anthropomorphic 118 119
application 32 33 42 43 74
archive 89 91 100 101
ariadne´s thread 15
atmosphere 62
audio 138 139
avatar 118 121

B

babyfaces 146 147
background colour 62
battle ships 83
bayeux tapestry 38 39
book 16 17 96 99
bookmark 15 17 90 91
boolean operation 80
brand emblems 65
bread crumbs 15
browser 22 23 46
browser setting 47
browser skin 22
button 42 43 56 57 113

C

calculation 42 43
colour coding 34 35 46 72 73
comic 65
complexity 53 72
computer 30 31 42 43
confusion 85
context 36 41 130 131
continuous scale 40
corporate identity 62
cross-index 72
cross-media 26 27 140 141
cursor 31 52 113
cyberspace 122
cyberworld 120 121

D

database 19 74 82 142 143
desktop metaphor 112 113 115
digital companion 118 119
direct manipulation 30 33 112 113
disorientation 122 123
display sizes 38 39 52 53 130 146 148
distorted zoom 40
drafting assistant 30
drag and drop 112

E

e-commerce 96 97 104 105 118 142 143
e-mail 94 95
e-paper 67 98 99
emoticons 94 95 110
entertainment value 87
experimental 130 135 138 141

F

feedback 32 33 58 59 134 135 138 139
Flash 50 134 135
font 46 47 137
frames 48
framework 38 41 114 115
function 42 56

G

games 118 122 123
guided tours 24 25

H

handwriting 94 95 148
hierarchy 40 48
hieroglyphs 65
home 22 23
home page 62 63
host 78 81
hotelling 149
HTML 46 47
hyperlinks 16 34 35
hypertext 34 35 85

I

icons 64 65 110 111
illusion 42 43 56 57
i-mode 147
implementation 74
instruction 110 113
intelligent products 152 153
interaction 30 33 112 113 134 135 140 141 148 149
interface 30 148 149
Internet Explorer 22 23
intuitive operation 30 31 112 113 126 127
IP number 18

L

layout 47
links 34 35 46
loading 58 59 87
location-based services 150 151

M

mail 94 95
manipulation 30 112
map 14 15 68 69
mapping information 68 73
marking 14 15
memory 36 37 66 89
mental models 34 35 110 111
menu 48 53 116 117
metaphor 112 115
metasearch 79
migration 146 149
misinterpretation 84
mnemonic 66 112
mobile internet 146 151
mosaic 22 23
multimedia 70 75 138 139

1 2 3 4 5 6 7 8 9

What is Navigation?
Navigation through Interaction
Archetypes and Stereotypes
Cognition and Recognition
Search Engines versus Serendipity
The Parallel Universe
Mental Models, Metaphors and Cyberworlds
New Frontiers
What's Next?

R

random	86	87	141	143
raw data	73			
reaction	32			
real time	32	33 74	75	120
recognition	66	69		
reduction	136			
redundancy	89			
repeat visit	87	90	91	
resolution	70	98	146	
roll-over menu	53			

N

navigable movie	124	127		
Netscape Navigator	22	23		
network	18	21		
networked products	26	27	152	

O

orientation	14	19		
	107	116	138	34
overview	40	41 71	122	123

P

page number	16			
pan	40	41	150	
panoramic picture	124	125		
parchment role	46			
pattern recognition	66	67		
PDA	114	115 148	150	
PDF	98	99		
personalisation	87	141		
personification	118	121		
pictograms	64	67		
pixel	136			
plausibility	40	41		
playground	132	133		
point and click	113			
pop-up menu	53			
portal	24	25	102	
positioning	150	151		
programing	74	75		
pull-down menu	53			

Q

Quicktime Player	43			
Quicktime VR	124	127		

S

scalable				
applications	146	149		
scanning	63			
scrollbar	36	37		
scrolling	38	39 46	151	
search	89			
search behavior	78	81	84	
search engine	84	85		
search query	78	104		
serendipity	86	87		
shopping cart	110	111		
signposts	64	65		
simulation	74	122		
site maps	54	55 83	89	
site search	82	83		
smart phone	149			
SMS	140	141	146	
software prototype	148	151		
sound	138	139		
speed	32	33	148	
spatial memory	36	122		
spatial metaphor	112	117		
strolling	89	97		
surfing	86	87	91	
symbolic actions	112			
symbols	64	65 110	111	
synchronous				
optical presentation	40	41 70	71	98

T

tabloid newspaper	63	100	101			
tags	46					
television	102	103				
text	63	67	98	99		
three-dimensional	36	85 120	121	126	127	
thumbnails	36	66 67	90	91	96	
time line	38	39 130	131	143		
tools	110					
top level domain	18	21				
transmission rate	32	33 58	148			
tree structure	36	37				

U

URL	18	19 22	62	

V

vector	57	134	
virtual	120		
	127		
virtual physics	134	135	
virtual reality	124	125	
visit	62	63	
visualisation	68		
	75	104	151
visual language	136	137	
visual perception	70	73	

W

WAP	146		
wearable computer	152	153	
web culture	142	143	
web design	47		

Z

zoom	40	41 98	142	